Praise for *As Ohio Goes*

"Every four years, Ohio becomes a political battleground for presidential candidates, who talk a lot and pretend to listen. Rana Khoury's captivating first book, *As Ohio Goes,* offers a much-needed corrective. Curious and intrepid, Khoury traveled the state for a year and has returned with stories of working men and women that are at once illuminating, heartbreaking, and inspiring. There are no easy answers found here. But if we listen to the voices that Khoury has captured, we will find plenty of hard-earned wisdom that can point the way forward."—**Gabriel Thompson**, author of *America's Social Arsonist: Fred Ross and Grassroots Organizing in the Twentieth Century*

"Rana Khoury spent a year traveling through her native state, talking with ordinary Ohioans about how the Great Recession has ravaged their lives. The result is a devastating indictment of a society in deep economic crisis. It is an unsettling and important read."—**Perry Bush**, author of *Rust Belt Resistance: How a Small Community Took On Big Oil and Won* (The Kent State University Press, 2012)

"The voices of the people Rana Khoury has included need to be heard. Policy makers deal with statistics. They need to 'see' the people behind them. This book takes them to that place."—**Dale Maharidge**, author of *Someplace Like America: Tales from the New Great Depression*

"I recommend *As Ohio Goes* to anyone who wants to understand the hopes, fears, anguish, and heartbreak being experienced by so many of our citizens. Rana B. Khoury writes so beautifully of average people caught up in the maelstrom of an economy in transition. She's traveled throughout Ohio—listening to the stories of people from diverse backgrounds who are struggling in this post-recession economy to provide a decent life for themselves and their loved ones. What I found most amazing about this book is the way Rana makes it comfortable for people to share the most intimate details of their lives. As you read their stories, it becomes impossible to hide from the reality of life in America today. If you want a deeper understanding of America and the struggles of its people, I urge you to read *As Ohio Goes*."—**Ted Strickland, 68th Governor of Ohio**

As Ohio Goes

Life in the Post-Recession Nation

Rana B. Khoury

The Kent State University Press ⊠ Kent, Ohio

© 2016 by The Kent State University Press, Kent, Ohio 44242

All rights reserved

Library of Congress Catalog Number 2015036102

ISBN 978-1-60635-280-9

Manufactured in the United States of America

LIBRARY OF CONGRESS CATALOGING-IN-PUBLICATION DATA

Names: Khoury, Rana B., author.

Title: As Ohio goes : life in the post-recession nation / Rana B. Khoury.

Description: Kent, Ohio : Kent State University Press, [2016] | Includes bibliographi-
cal references and index.

Identifiers: LCCN 2015036102 | ISBN 9781606352809 (pbk. : alk. paper) ∞

Subjects: LCSH: Working class--Ohio. | Ohio--Economic conditions--21st century.
| Ohio--Social conditions--21st century. | Recessions--Social aspects--United
States--History--21st century. | United States--Politics and government--2009-

Classification: LCC HD8083.O3 K46 2016 | DDC 330.9771--dc23

LC record available at http://lccn.loc.gov/2015036102

20 19 18 17 16   5 4 3 2 1

To my parents

Contents

Acknowledgments

Each time I listen to someone's life story, I feel part of a precious undertaking. I am a stranger being entrusted with private sentiments. I know my probing exposes weaknesses and fears. Occasionally, the whole process creates a sense of hope, the prospect of making a difference lingering enticingly over the conversation. Carrying the weight of these stories is sometimes overwhelming and at all times humbling. To those Ohioans who shared their stories—thank you. You have made this book possible. You have also made my life more meaningful.

I did not take on this task without assistance. In Ohio I benefited greatly from the guidance and hospitality of people in each corner of the state—Greg Miller, Richey Piiparinen, Beth Swartz, and George Windau. Sherry Linkon and John Russo, founders and longtime directors of the eminent Center for Working-Class Studies at Youngstown State University, advised me as if I were one of their students. Ann Harris and Paul Bellamy helped me understand, and thereby relay, specialized issues.

Although this project was well under way before I arrived at Northwestern University, once there I benefited from the input of Jordan Gans-Morse and Benjamin Iverson, as well as from support from the American Politics program in the Political Science Department. I am especially grateful to Benjamin I. Page. His reading and feedback on particular chapters was of great value; his professorship and scholarship, even more so. Several others have read portions of the project out of no obligation to me but their friendship: Anny Gaul, Scott Kroehle, Thomas Osann, and Jason Paul.

All that input and assistance helped produce a manuscript that Joyce Harrison of Kent State University Press deemed worth publishing. I'm grateful to her for taking a chance on me, to the rest of the staff at KSUP for working toward publication, and to Marian Buda for making the book a more readable final product.

There are a handful of individuals whose reading of my manuscript has been just a small part of their contributions to my life. Dale Maharidge was my teacher before he even met me; since our meeting in New York, he may have sealed his place as my role model for good. Michael C. Hudson is a master of mentoring. From Georgetown to Singapore, he has enlightened me on everything from Arab politics and foreign policy to gin martinis and impressionism. Alex Shakar excites my mind with his writing and intellect; he soothes my heart with his love and equanimity. Alex is my good luck. Finally, I thank my parents, Wael and Sawssan Khoury. They have encouraged my various undertakings generously and persistently. More importantly, they are the ones who implanted in me the unrelenting desire to see, experience, and understand the world around me. They also created a family—which includes my siblings Shaadi, Hala, and Leila—that is a constant source of support and love.

CHAPTER ONE

As Ohio Goes

"It doesn't affect us as much because we don't have the overhead like you people do, as far as no electric bill, no mortgage. No, just the business."

I sat on a stiff couch across the room from Jacob,* who was swaying on one of three wooden rocking chairs padded with blue quilted cushions. A ceiling-high wooden chest with glass doors stood between two windows that cast bright sunlight onto the living room's glossy wooden floor. A few other wooden tables filled the spaces in the room, each boasting a distinct design. On one wall hung an Ohio-shaped clock with each county in the state inlaid in a different color of wood; I was east of 3 o'clock, in Carroll County, home to one of the region's Amish communities. Jacob had built everything I was looking at.

Toward the end of our conversation, Jacob brought into the room a musical contraption he had made: a large steel tub turned open-side down, fitted with a wooden bow and a thick string. Jacob hung a harmonica holder on his shoulders, freeing his hands to pluck the instrument while blowing and sucking a folk tune on the mouth organ for the next ten minutes. It was a researcher's paradise.

Still, my mind was stuck on that earlier sentence. Here in front of me was someone unaffected by the Great Recession. And all that

---

*Jacob is not the real name of this speaker. Throughout the book, to preserve the privacy of certain people I have interviewed, I have substituted pseudonyms for their real names; this will be indicated by an asterisk after each pseudonym on first mention.

took was living in the middle of nowhere, forgoing public services in favor of his community's schools and health care, relying extensively on his neighbors and himself for food, water, and shelter, and believing wholeheartedly in a Dutch-speaking god whose first day of work forever obviated the need for electricity.

Or so it seemed.

Like his father, Jacob's oldest son was in the sawmill business. Dependent as lumber is on the construction of new property, they had both felt the burst of the housing bubble in 2007. But the son's livelihood was more severely affected because he also had money in real estate. "One thing led to another . . . things got so bad," Jacob hesitantly recalled of his son's experience. The son began selling off properties at a great loss while battling problems at home: financial stress was destroying his marriage. After two difficult years, he decided to leave. That is, he left his family and the church; he would no longer be Amish. He went up to Maine without his wife and their children, though they remain married nonetheless. "They're not divorced," Jacob declares: "wedding vows are till death." Leaving the community is not uncommon, Jacob admits. "But we never expected it to be one of our own children."

I'd call that an effect.

.   .   .

Recessions happen. Indeed, they occur almost every decade. Fortunately, the fluctuations that are a natural part of modern economies are marked by more ups than downs. But the recession that officially began in December 2007 and ended in June 2009 was different for two reasons. First, it was *Great*. Persisting for eighteen months, it was our longest recession since the Second World War. In October 2008, the Dow Jones experienced its worst weekly loss in history. Two months later, the Federal Reserve lowered interest rates to zero—an institutional first. That year, the federal government bailed out the economy by spending hundreds of billions of dollars more than ever before. By the close of 2008, unemployment had increased in every single state in the union for the first time since such records have been kept. *After* the official end of the recession, the unemployment rate reached double digits for the first time in a quarter of a century. From 2009 to 2010, Americans experienced their largest single-year decline in income in more than forty years. More Americans were living in poverty than had done so in nearly twenty years. More than four years after the recession's end, participation in the labor force was at its lowest point in more than four decades. It's no surprise that *Great* is widely used as an epithet for this event, but I think *Catastrophic Recession* and *Record-Breaking Recession* are equally apt labels.

A second reason this recession was different from the usual economic fluctuations—and the reason the stories in this book are not limited to the crisis itself—is that it was part of a long-term process that was already under way and continues unabated. Escalating inequality and declining standards of living define this process; the rich are gaining while most Americans are stuck, or worse. This book tells the stories of the "most"—that is, of those Americans who have been living what George Packer has vividly called "the unwinding," a metaphorical unraveling of financial security, public infrastructure, personal dreams, and community cohesion.[1] It refers to that uncomfortable sense that a secure life is hard to hold on to these days.

The term *unwinding* is useful because it alludes to something more than decline; it captures a transformation that is not always directed downward. Life in America is not uniformly marked by descent. But society is changing in profound ways, and we are sometimes slow to adjust. For instance, more women than ever are breadwinners, contributing the primary or sole income to their households. Yet policies for maternal leave have scarcely changed. Another example is the rise in educational attainment; more Americans than ever are receiving college educations, yet unsustainable levels of student debt offset this positive development.

The stories you will encounter in these pages speak to these transformations and others. Not all of them chronicle decline. Indeed,

I assure you that at least some of the stories will inspire hope. My objective is to reveal the dynamism of life in America, rather than to paint a uniformly dark picture. To do so would be misleading. Yet clearly, other aspects of the transformation are deeply problematic. One is wage stagnation. After rising steadily since World War II, American wages began to stagnate and even decrease in the 1980s. Wages ticked back up in the 1990s, and by 2002 the median worker in Ohio was making $16.62 per hour (still less than in 1979). Decline followed again, and ten years later a median Ohio worker was making $15.54 an hour (figures adjusted for inflation). In some parts of the country, workers enjoyed more consistent wage increases, so that overall Americans' median wages increased by about 80 cents between 1979 and 2012.[2] But a closer look reveals that among men alone median wages declined uniformly and that workers below the median have suffered more severe wage decreases.

Let's zoom out instead. Total household income usually includes more than one person's wages; within a family, for example, it includes the earnings of multiple members. In this context, the total income of the median American family increased by 20 percent from 1990 to 2008—yet over the same period, the costs of basic "middle class items" rose by much more: housing by 56 percent, four-year public college by 60 percent, and health care by a staggering 155 percent (all adjusted for inflation).[3] Likewise, although labor productivity—the output of workers—was also increasing,[4] worker output failed to translate into worker payback.

This kind of statistical context frames all the stories that follow. But this book is more concerned with narratives than with numbers. Many elements of the unwinding cannot be understood except through a reading of human experiences. Faith in the American Dream, for instance, cannot be precisely quantified. Though never perfectly or equally realizable for all, the American Dream has always been at the heart of our national project, bringing generations of immigrants to our shores and allowing native and foreign-born inhabitants alike to forge their own destinies—at least more so than almost anywhere else in the world. Yet the core tenets of the American Dream—that hard work is rewarded and that real opportunities exist for upward mobility—are now strained at best, outmoded myths at worst.

People's histories can also unearth intimate sentiments. Feelings like disempowerment and frustration, and perceptions of unfairness and inequity are widely felt but often unspoken. Similarly, evidence of perseverance and of attachments to work, family, and faith is most accessible through trustful conversations. Common classifications—including "middle class," "working poor," and even "poverty"—are fluctuating and subjective, eluding precise definition. Looking closely into the lives of others allows us a better sense of what it means to inhabit these categories, and whether people defy them or submit to them. Herein is the purpose of this book: to reveal life in the post-recession United States in human terms.

. . .

Before traveling to Ohio, let us briefly survey the long-term escalation of inequality in America. The stories of the super rich are not told in this book, but we cannot afford to ignore their existence. Income inequality has tangible effects on everyday lives and on the country as a whole. That was certainly true of the Great Recession, which was catalyzed and exacerbated by the low spending power of average Americans. Prior to it, economic demand was limited except for housing—then that bubble burst. During the recovery, spending remained low, so unemployment remained high.[5] Inequality also unhinges values we associate with democracy, like fairness, access, and equalities of opportunity and representation. The exceptional gains of some Americans necessarily affect the economic and political lives of all Americans.

So what do those gains look like? The Great Recession, and the Occupy Wall Street movement it provoked, alerted many people to the growing gap in prosperity between the 99 percent and the 1 percent of Americans. The income earners and wealth holders making up the top 1 percent fall along a wide spectrum, but most of their riches are held by a mere fraction of their ranks. For simplicity we will treat them as one. With their income defined to include market income and "realized" capital gains, they earned $400,000 or more in 2012. On the eve of the recession in 2007, that small group of people enjoyed over one-fifth of the nation's income. Together with the 9 percent of earners just below them, they commanded nearly half of the total personal income in the United States. It wasn't always this way. In 2012, Americans in the top 10 percent enjoyed a larger share of the national income than they had in any year since 1917![6] The Great Depression that began in 1929 then accentuated the imbalances; the Second World War attenuated them. In the decades that followed, income became more widely distributed as a new middle class emerged and took a big piece of the pie. By the 1960s and '70s, the top 1 percent and the top 10 percent of Americans held, respectively, a relatively modest 9 percent and 33 percent of total income.[7] In the 1980s, however, while average Americans' incomes were stagnating, the fortunes of the rich began to increase dramatically and have continued to enjoy big gains through 2015. By 2030, if this pattern were to continue at its current pace, the top 10 percent of U.S. income earners could command 60 percent of all national income.[8]

Moreover, the rich are not making more money in isolation; their gains often come at the expense of everyone else. From 1993 to 2012, the "average" (mean) real income of an American family grew by 18 percent. But removing the top 1 percent from the picture brings the percentage of growth down from 18 to 6.6 percent. Put another way, 99 percent of Americans saw their incomes grow by less than 7 percent over two decades, while over the same period, the top 1 percent of Americans enjoyed income growth of an amazing 86 percent.[9]

How have top income earners managed to do so well? We can locate key processes from the global level down to the individual. Economic globalization has opened pools of cheap labor around the world that compete with—and drive down the wages of—workers in advanced countries like the United States. Meanwhile, governments vie with one another to entice investment by reducing their tax rates. Globalizing forces also favor technical and skilled labor at home, raising the value of the work of the highly educated.[10] In Washington, D.C., politicians seem to be aligned with business interests. They preside over policies like the dismantling of financial regulations and the reduction of top tax rates. This might be the result of purposeful policymaking, or it might be (conscious) neglect; either way, the government is allowing business interests to gain in both power and riches.[11] Among individuals in the corporate world, lower tax rates have encouraged a transformation in norms related to bargaining practices and individualized pay for "supermanagers," who now fill the ranks of the top 1 percent and top 0.1 percent of earners.[12] To secure these gains, the super rich enlist a "wealth defense industry" of lawyers, accountants, lobbyists, and wealth management firms that generate lower published tax rates, push tax burdens downward on the income scale, and maintain a special, low rate for capital gains.[13]

These processes necessarily overlap, and all seem to be at play. But a fixation on the global level alone often becomes a pretext for acquiescence. National and individual actors *do* have some power to either enable or soften the impact of global processes. Throughout this book, I take opportunities to point out the intersection of these global processes with national policies. In the concluding chapter, I will return to this question to examine how policy outcomes reflect the interests of the wealthy rather than those of average citizens.

To be fair, during the Great Recession (as has been the case during all downturns), top earners did lose out at even higher rates than everyone else. Yet they made up for their losses—and then some—during the economic recovery. From 2009 to 2012, Americans' average real incomes grew by about 6 percent. Once again when we break it down, we find that the incomes of 99 percent of people grew by only 0.4 percent, while those of the top 1 percent of Americans grew by more than 30 percent. In other words, the affluent captured 95 percent of all income growth in the first three years after the recession ended.[14] Stark patterns likewise emerge when we break these figures down by race. Before the recession, white households had ten times more median wealth than blacks; in 2013, they had thirteen times more. The gap in wealth between whites and Hispanics is likewise expanding.[15]

Through good economic times and despite the bad, a small group of Americans has been enjoying the nation's economic growth much more than everyone else. Even with increased attention and anger in the wake of the crisis, income inequality remains a matter of fact in the post-recession United States.

. . .

Some economists have grasped the gravity of these developments and are addressing the complexities involved, often in quite illuminating ways.[16] I am not one of them. This book endeavors to put a human face on issues that economic experts deal with in the abstract. I want to pump blood into otherwise cold facts and figures. In part, my desire to do so comes from noticing that most writing about the crisis has lacked the human factor. Additionally, six years of living in Washington, D.C., left me with the strong impression that the people who make our national decisions have scant idea of how people outside the Beltway are living. Ultimately, the gravity of the circumstances is reason enough to pursue this project. The most astounding economic crisis since the Great Depression demands historical documentation through real people's histories. From 2012 through 2013, therefore, I returned home to Ohio and drove around the state listening to people's stories. Now I want to tell them.

Although not everyone I spoke to appears in these pages, the words of all informed my understanding of the "unwinding" in its various manifestations. I have organized the stories into broad thematic chapters (a challenging task, considering that the dynamic individuals I interviewed could easily traverse and transcend my themes). Each chapter contains a handful of people's stories, told within a broader social, historical, and statistical context that serves both to deepen our understanding of their personal experiences and to extend and relate them to the wider population. In closing each chapter, I suggest a general way to think about the stories just told.

In chapter 2, we will meet manufacturing and automotive workers who have spent decades in industrial plants. Some recently lost their jobs, while others held on tightly to their labor unions and, at times, their religions. The subjects in chapter 3 all lost jobs or income during the crisis. Most found a way back onto their feet, although their balance may be wobbly. Chapter 4 reveals how working women have supported themselves and their families, each navigating her own path between livelihood and motherhood, unassisted by a marked road even in the age of female breadwinners. The generation these women are bringing up is the subject of chapter 5, where we meet indebted students, scarred soldiers, and a fledgling businessman. Through their stories, we witness the precarious nature of young adulthood in insecure times but also an indefatigable determination to get by at all times. Chapter 6 chronicles a journey through Ohio's farmlands, sprouting lucratively subsidized crops and unprofitable organics, and extracting shale gas to boot. No one image captures the American farmer today, although tireless work is shared by all. In chapter 7, we encounter people trying to embody that other idealized image: the American homeowner. Their struggles to pay for health insurance and mortgages put the notion of healthy citizenship to the test. Finally, in my conclusion, I step back from individual stories to investigate the political consequences of inequality. I also suggest that party politics is the wrong lens to use for assessing "divisions" in a bellwether state like Ohio.

My method can be summed up rather simply: I asked folks to talk to me. This book is not exactly a scholarly production—and it is not meant to be. The scientific approach is in my arsenal, but my overriding mission has been to keep the book accessible to all readers. My sampling of interview subjects was not totally random; I purposefully sought demographic and occupational diversity. That said, I did not seek out stories to fit any particular narrative, such as one of decline.

In fact, I frequently had to assure interviewees that I was interested in their story although they had kept their jobs or homes. Most often, I found that people were happy to talk; they were usually delighted that somebody cared enough to listen. Nor is this work a feat of immersion journalism or participant observation. Even so, I went to my interviewees. I ate more corn dogs and fried pickles at county fairs than I care to remember; I consumed just enough beer at local pubs so as not to forget; and I muddied up a few pairs of shoes in lumber yards, rows of planted fields, and industrial plant ruins. People took me into their homes and their workplaces, and they spoke to me in (sometimes surprising) detail about their past experiences and personal grievances. I followed up with many of them and remain in regular contact with a few. But each interview had an end, and I always had the luxury of traveling home to an environment that allowed me to write about my encounters.

The reader will note that this text covers a larger range of topics than a single scholar could command in depth. Yet a diligent writer can say something useful about each of them. A host of sources has helped provide context. Government agencies like the Bureau of Labor Statistics and the Census Bureau collect and maintain immense amounts of data enumerating patterns of American life; state-level agencies similarly produce vast quantities of information on their states' inhabitants. Countless research institutes and polling organizations also seek to capture America in numbers and often do so in creative, if sometimes partial, ways. I sought the advice of scholars who shed light on areas in which I could not hope to be an expert. I have consulted all of these resources eagerly and with an eye to scientific merit.

. . .

The old adage tells us that "As Ohio goes, so goes the nation." If it is right, then Ohio's stories should give us a view of America's prospects. Most people pay attention to the state during national election season, and with good reason. With its eighteen Electoral College votes, Ohio is a "swing state" in the sense that it can pull one or the other of the presidential candidates over the top of the 270 votes needed for victory. California has triple the number of Electoral College votes, but they are practically given to the Democrats, who must accumulate more elsewhere. The same goes for a state like Texas, a reliable source of votes for the Republican count. Ohio, on the other hand, is both less predictable and more predictive. Ohioans have voted for the winner in every presidential election but two since 1904.

While this status is empowering for individual voters in Ohio, the electioneering it brings into the state can be patronizing and polarizing. During the three nights of the Democratic National Convention in 2012, Ohio was mentioned more than thirty times. And if Ohioans weren't watching the party conventions, they were still on the receiving end of an unprecedented four hundred television ads per day, or sixteen per hour, during that campaign season.[17] One of the two presidential candidates visited the state almost every week.

The candidates in 2012 offered different visions for America's future, indeed, two distinct understandings of the country's very nature. From the Democrats, we heard of government that works to improve the condition of all Americans, while the Republicans disparaged government and insisted they would empower individuals to improve their own lot. Vice President Joe Biden claimed that he did not "recognize Mitt Romney's America," while Romney's vice presidential candidate, Paul Ryan, declared that Barack Obama's idea of governance was "entirely foreign to anything this nation has ever known."[18] Two Americas, they told us. Choose one.

The disagreements are real. On the ground, activists were engaged in the same battles that consumed politicians and pundits. Traveling through Ohio in the fall of 2012, I witnessed plenty of acrimony. In one instance, Tea Party followers rallied in downtown Cleveland, declaring war.† One volunteer, an elderly woman with a sweet

†The activists borrowed the term war from the late conservative journalist Andrew Breitbart.

demeanor, kindly told me, "November is going to be do or die." I raised my eyes from my notebook and met hers, engulfed in wrinkles that turned upward as she smiled. Earlier that year, five young men loosely affiliated with Occupy Cleveland were arrested after an FBI sting operation ensnared them in a bomb plot. Meanwhile, Governor John Kasich's administration was occupied by its efforts to restrict early voting, a program with racially discriminatory consequences, if not motivations. The policy was fought out—and defeated—at the national level, first at the U.S. District Court and then at the U.S. Court of Appeals for the Sixth Circuit; the Supreme Court declined to hear the appeal, leaving the polls open.

This spectacle is likely to repeat itself every four years: the campaigns will descend on Ohio, the advertisements will flood through homes, polarization and negativity will prevail, and the world will watch intently. The main difference is that more campaign money will be spent each time.

Yet the image of a state of indecisive voters in need of convincing is rather misleading. We Ohioans swing because we are diverse, not because we can't make up our minds. Blue and red do not capture Ohio's character. The lake to our north and the river encircling us reflect the grey smoke puttering from industrial plants. In the east, the verdant hills of Appalachia boast a beauty that hides the blackened coal mines beneath them. South and west are patches of yellows, fields growing the grains found in our children's bagged lunches and in the feedstock of Chinese pigs. Cleveland hosts one of the world's top medical centers; Columbus, one of the country's biggest universities; and Cincinnati, enough religion to keep us firmly rooted in the American Midwest. Blemishes mark the landscape, too. On election night 2012, Americans stared at their television sets as the areas marking Cuyahoga County (home to Cleveland) turned blue enough to call the election for Barack Obama; those digital maps didn't capture a region dogged by foreclosure. Youngstown remains in the grip of a deindustrialization process that refuses to let the city recover. Systemic racial injustices are perpetrated from above: during election season, billboards warning of the frightening consequences of voter fraud were displayed *exclusively* in poor urban neighborhoods. These are the reasons Ohio swings. We are world class and we are grit, we are every occupation and we are unemployed, we are diversity and we are prejudice—we are America.

CHAPTER TWO

The Company Is Your Family

> There is nothing better for a man, than that he should
> eat and drink, and that he should make his soul enjoy
> good in his labor.
> —Ecclesiastes 2:24

I'm from this little town, raised here all my life. I'm disabled right now, but I worked at a refractory plant for almost thirty-eight years. I used to run the forklift and load and unload trucks. Stopped in 2006. My lungs, I got silicosis in my lungs. And I can't, I can't go very far. I have a hard time breathing. I was coming up on retirement. I'm getting disability and social security. We've had a few rough times because of the high price of our medication. And we sent our son through college. But we still . . . we have managed . . . because we watch what we're doing and what we're spending. Some things we would like to do we do not do anymore. We used to love to go and play Bingo. Used to play it three or four nights and we had to cut it out because everything kind of went down. We had to be careful.

My wife, she's disabled too. She was a nurse for twenty-five years. We have one child, twenty-two. He just graduated from college. He double-majored in economics and business administration. He was at the top of his class, and received five awards from the college. He hasn't had no work or any offers until just last week. Last week he was very fortunate to get two phone calls for interviews. And we're hoping that everything works out for him.

I consider myself middle class. We're not poor because I've seen too many people who don't have anything. I have my home, and we have our vehicle. All of our life we've been very careful with how we handled everything, our situations and finances. I have a very wonderful wife who sometimes says, "No, we can't do that, we have to be careful."

The refractory plant is a very good place to work. And they tried to do the best they can for their men. Sometimes, it's hard for both situations: for the men and the company. But they have been kept open and kept everybody busy. We have a union, United Steel Workers. We had a pension plan. We worked and we had vacations. We had paid holidays. We got paid overtime for after eight hours. A couple of times we had to give in, too. We had to have a two-tier for a while, which we didn't like but we did 'cause we wanted to keep the company going. But now the company is back to just one wage because they were able to work together and everybody is doing just fine right now. They have good benefits for the men. And one of the biggest reasons they have that is because they have families too and they realize that the men have to have hospitalization and stuff. And I think it's both union and the company working together. It's been very good.

—Gary, 63

Gary* spoke slowly, gently carrying each word out of his mind and into its place in our conversation. Though it had come to him early, he wore retirement comfortably, in a tie-dye T-shirt, blue jean shorts, and white face stubble. It was a blistering hot day; I found him seated on a park bench enjoying the shade. Sitting down, I wanted a share of the tree's shadow; I also hoped to speak to him. At times it was that easy to get a story; everyone has one, after all. When his wife was ready to leave, he apologized and joined her. I watched as they gradually disappeared: his slow gait, her rolling wheelchair.

Then I left, anxious to learn more about Gary's disability, silicosis. According to the American Lung Association, silicosis causes fluid buildup and scar tissue in the lungs. The disease commonly affects people who work where they may inhale tiny bits of silica.

Immediately looking up refractory plants, I discovered that silica is a core substance in refractory manufacturing. My mind darted back to Gary and I recalled the close of our conversation.

ME: Was your job ever physically risky?
GARY: Every day.
ME: But you were never affected? Never hurt?
GARY: No, no.

· · ·

When I met George in person for the first time, the energy I had detected in his e-mails was blazing. He had gathered four other autoworkers to join us for dinner at Big Boy's in Toledo. His flair for storytelling was the special sauce to our burgers and fries.

Gary came to mind when George declared that he would not stand for being put in danger at work. That resolve briefly lost him his job in 1977—his first year with Chrysler. Back then he was working on Jeep Cherokee tailgates that hung by hooks above the workers. Each tailgate weighed about seventy pounds, and a jerk in the line could cause the hooks to break, sending those metal hunks tumbling down onto the men below. George, with the audacity of a rookie, demanded that a safety cage be placed below the tailgates. Instead, management handed over a single hard hat, apparently to be shared among the four men on the floor. Some days later, a tailgate fell, landing six inches in front of George—Boom! The crash set George off. He shut down the line, nailed his union card to the wall, and declared he would retrieve the card and resume working only if and when the situation was addressed. The plant manager asked George if he was refusing to work. When George defiantly said yes, the manager called in a replacement. Ignited beyond containment, George picked up his hammer and threatened, "Anyone who's gonna come do this job is gonna go through this hammer!" Security guards swept in and escorted him out of the building.

Witnesses to the episode, George's fellow workers initiated a wildcat strike. They informed management that if the safety issue was not addressed by the following week, they would not return to work. The strike succeeded. That weekend, the company installed seventy-five feet of safety cage, and the men returned to the line. Three months later, George did too. He had taken his case to the National Labor Relations Board, which awarded him back pay and reinstatement. He particularly enjoyed the ninety-day posting of a public apology on the bulletin boards in the plant.

Three decades after his rebellion, when he told me his tale, George was still an employee of Chrysler and a member of the United Auto Workers (UAW). By his lights, the two—work and labor activism—are inseparable. After graduating from Ohio State University, where he was a self-professed "campus radical," George ran out of money. He applied for the job at Chrysler as a way to pay the bills. On arriving at the plant on his first day, he found his new colleagues outside the main gate drinking beers. When he asked what was going on, they told him that they "hit the bricks" to protest a safety issue. Apparently, a millwright had been up on a ladder when the boss started up the assembly line beneath him; the automobile on the line hit the ladder and knocked it down, leaving the man holding on for his life above the moving line. The workers stopped the assembly line, brought the man down to safety, and then called a wildcat strike. George looked around him and thought, "So all these guys are drinking beer, having a wildcat strike, and I says, 'This is the job for me! This is where I belong!'"

He knew at that moment that he would be active in the union, a commitment he kept. Among other organizing activities, George participated in a buyout committee that bid to make Chrysler an employee-owned corporation in 2006. (The committee established a line of credit, but the effort failed because, George contends, "they're not going to let these major automobile companies become employee-owned any more than they would let the slaves own a plantation in Georgia.") Occasionally George had union experiences that "were not so good" because of his tendency to make trouble; lightheartedly, he mentions that at one union meeting he was knocked unconscious. It's not hard to imagine why "some people wanted to kick [his] ribs in at meetings." George is charismatic, outspoken, humorous, intelligent, and politicized. Those characteristics made him threatening to some. They also made him popular among most. When I started my search for autoworkers to speak to in Toledo, it did not take long for me to hear about George.

Perhaps that's because George resembles Toledo. His face is an inviting kind of handsome, topped with thick brown hair surrendering slowly to white, entering into a distinguished maturity. The city wears its age in a similar fashion. Toledo is an old manufacturing town made beautiful by the wide Maumee River rolling through, flowing into the bay and out to Lake Erie, a mosaic of blues and greens. Just behind the trendy waterfront restaurants are the industrial plants; just below George's fashionable fisherman's hat is the dirt beneath his fingernails. Donning a denim shirt with his worn jeans, George's person is literally blue-collar.

If northwestern Ohio could wear a collar, it would be blue too. With Toledo at its heart, the region contains about one-fifth of Ohio's total manufacturing industry, the largest share in the state.[1] Manufacturing predominates statewide, too. One out of every five dollars earned in private-sector wages in Ohio is made in the manufacturing industry, constituting the largest share of total private wages in 2011. Moreover, Ohio's industrial activity moves the nation. The state ranks second in the country in the manufacturing of primary and fabricated metals and third in motor-vehicle production.[2]

Industry around here used to be even bigger. In 1970, nearly one and a half million Ohioans worked in manufacturing. By 1990, the number was down to about one million. The next two decades saw a commensurate loss, leaving fewer than seven hundred thousand Ohioans working in the sector by 2012.[3] The decline is national, of course: between 1970 and 2005, the United States lost 20 percent of manufacturing jobs. But in Toledo's Lucas County, manufacturing jobs declined by 54 percent. And while the nation made up for its manufacturing losses in other sectors, total employment in Lucas County grew at just half the national rate. Given the auto industry's former predominance, George never could have fathomed its financial ruin. "When I was in my twenties, if somebody had said General Motors is going to go bankrupt, I would have said, 'I want a six pack of what you're drinking, because that's crazy!'"

Somebody get this man a beer.

The financial troubles of the "Big Three"—Ford, General Motors, and Chrysler—hit hard and fast. In spring 2008, gas prices climbed to new highs, access to credit evaded companies and consumers alike, and auto sales dropped to new lows. At GM, for example, sales in 2008 were down 16 percent from those of the previous year; by March 2009, they were down 53 percent from that low.[4] Assembly lines slowed or shut down altogether, plants closed, and workers lost their jobs—the lucky ones lost only their benefits. The car companies reached their nadir. But the real fear was whether the whole industry—perhaps the whole economy—might collapse. Should Chrysler or GM fail (both were in worse shape than Ford), their own job losses and those of other workers connected to the industry would cause national unemployment rates, already high, to soar. Ford's CEO, Alan Mulally, reflected that a total bankruptcy at GM or Chrysler might well have "turned the U.S. recession into a depression."[5] To prevent that outcome (and save themselves), the Big Three went to Washington to request government loans, first from Bush's administration and then from Obama's. On condition that the companies undertook substantial restructuring, Washington paid out to Detroit. GM and Chrysler filed bankruptcy and accepted sixty-four billion dollars in bailout funds, while Ford borrowed a more modest but still critical six billion dollars. Another twenty billion dollars went to the companies' affiliates.[6]

With billions at play and the structural integrity of the American economy in the balance, politicians and pundits eagerly offered their diagnoses and prognoses. The industry's decline was variously explained as the product of creative destruction, of excessive union activism, or of a lack of corporate innovation. The wisdom of the government's rescue plan was similarly touted and pouted. The issue reemerged as a central theme in the 2012 presidential campaign, by which time it was widely considered a success. Mitt Romney rued the day he penned the words, "Let Detroit Go Bankrupt," while Barack Obama boasted repeatedly that, thanks to him, "GM is alive and Bin Laden is dead."[7] At a cost of eighty-five billion dollars, the auto rescue saved upward of one million jobs and more than seven billion dollars in unemployment payouts and Social Security benefits, as well as preventing personal income losses of ninety-seven billion dollars.[8] Furthermore, within a few years, the government had recovered most of the money it had disbursed in loans and—surely eager to extract itself from the business of selling cars—had sold off its stock in the auto companies.

After the auto industry had hemorrhaged forty thousand jobs in just over a year, the bleeding stopped in Ohio. The government's rescue package arrived when employment in the state's manufacturing industry had hit a historic low. Over the following three years, tens of thousands of manufacturing jobs came back,[9] each one a boon.

.   .   .

Throughout the crisis, as colleagues and benefits fell away, Pam held on to her job at Chrysler; the impact wouldn't force her out for a few years yet. She had begun working at Chrysler in 1972, a teenager who had never left her hometown, Toledo. When she started, Pam was making nine dollars for every ten made by her male colleagues—standard company practice. That same year, she took a vacation and returned to find that "women's rights [had gone] into effect," suddenly making her wage equivalent to the men's. Perhaps in response, management assigned her one of the hardest jobs: putting on clutch pedals with massive cylinders. "They said if women want to work in factories, they're going to work in factories and do the same jobs as men. And I guess that's what we wanted," she recalled. "I didn't know it, I was just nineteen years old." Four decades have since passed; the woman sitting across the table from me retains little hint of that youthful innocence.

Despite the wage increase reluctantly granted Pam and her female colleagues, sexist attitudes and behavior persisted. Pictures of naked women adorned toolboxes, crude commentary was on offer at lunchtime, and women were assigned gendered tasks like sweeping while men took their breaks. More serious offenses, such as demands by bosses for sexual favors in exchange for promotions, were kept "hush-hush." Corporate policies and societal norms against discrimination were still years away. In this patriarchal environment, Pam remained reticent: "You didn't want to get involved, didn't want to make waves and lose your job." Eventually, in the late 1990s, company policies corrected most of these discriminatory behaviors. "You don't see anything like that anymore; they have a no-nonsense policy today." Pam loved her work throughout these changing times.

In fact, she fell in love at the plant. Thanks to women's liberation and management's retribution, Pam met her husband in the body shop where she was assigned heavy lifting. He was a union steward ten years her senior, making him just thirty years old. They remain married today. A long marriage is a lucky one, I'm told. George chimed in to alert me to one consequence of the grueling schedules common in the industry, namely, high divorce rates. The company prefers to pay employees overtime—lots of it even—because doing so remains cheaper than hiring more people who would demand full salary and benefits packages. Since long hours invariably and negatively affect social and family life, the company may have concluded that it is better to keep family out of the picture altogether. These days, when young people are hired in, the company no longer offers medical coverage to their spouses and children. "They don't want to give to the family because they don't want you to have a family—the company is your family," George deduces. "They want institutionalized people.

Family life is a distraction from work life—that's the corporate way of thinking." Corporate officials would be unlikely to corroborate such statements, but the validity of George's words is perhaps less important than the underlying mistrust they reveal.

Still, Pam loved her marriage and her labor alike, finding comfort in their shared features: the repetition of daily motions, the acclimation to each other's habits, and the passing of time together. Perhaps the most distinctive characteristic of the relationship with her labor is the long hours at the plant. Pam was at work more than home. The standard workday was ten hours, but most days required eleven, and as a team leader during the last several years, Pam put in yet another hour. Added to that, her commute was half an hour each way, coming altogether to thirteen hours per day, six days per week. Working at that rate for four decades, as she put it, "it's our life." She has no regrets. "You work on a line, do the same thing for every vehicle, for forty years. And you work with every walk of life, and you have to get along with each other. I've had a great life."

Pam wanted it to stay that way until retirement. But she didn't want retirement to come early. The end began in 2006, when Jeep developed its third generation Wrangler. In an experimental mood, Chrysler (at that time DaimlerChrysler) decided to have the cars built on-site in Toledo, but with each plant operated by an outside supplier—one each to paint, build truck bodies, and assemble the vehicles. Chrysler may have intended the experiment to demonstrate higher efficiency to its stakeholders: because Chrysler would directly employ fewer of the laborers, more vehicles would be produced in apparently fewer labor hours. Yet when Chrysler sought to staff the paint shop from its ranks, management met a challenge—none of the workers wanted to risk their job security with Chrysler by becoming employees of a small operator. Moving its search up the ranks by seniority, Chrysler finally made an offer to those with more than thirty years of experience: if you go over to the Jeep Wrangler paint shop, we will retire you now and start paying your pension, plus the new operator will compensate you at your current hourly wage. Retiring early meant a lower pension for the future and leaving Chrysler meant less job security. Yet continuing to work at the same pay was something, at least. And Chrysler was persistent. "HR called me for four months to retire and come work there," Pam explains. "I said no until the very last day." Finally, she and more than seventy others went to the paint shop.

The first paint shop operator, Haden, went bankrupt quickly. Chrysler bought the facility and contracted with another operator, Magna International. In the coming years, Pam and her colleagues were affected by the economic crisis like everyone else. When Chrysler filed for Chapter 11 bankruptcy in 2009 and the government-mandated restructuring began, budget cuts or freezes targeted overtime pay, cost-of-living increases, medical and retirement benefits, and wages. Also as part of the restructuring, the American and Canadian governments and the Italian automaker Fiat acquired Chrysler's shareholdings, and in 2011 Fiat became a majority owner of Chrysler. A year later, Chrysler completely took over the paint shop from Magna (a known rival of Fiat)—operation, site, and employees. The experiment was over.

Time then, for the retirees to go.

When Chrysler took over the operation, Pam and her retired co-workers were told they could not become Chrysler employees again. Who would replace them? Younger workers, who make about half their hourly wages and lack the benefits of their seasoned colleagues. To Bruce Baumhower, president of the United Auto Workers Local 12, this was clearly a "money grab by the corporation to get rid of them and hire everybody in at tier-two wages."[10] To the workers, that injury was exacerbated by the cold hostility of protocol. Pam's colleague Beth recounted the sequence of events for me:

> We walked in one day in August this year and were told that in two weeks we no longer had a job. But since they didn't go by the right procedure, they had to give another sixty-day notice. Our [local union] committee was not allowed to negotiate with

the international [UAW] on our behalf. They weren't allowed in any of the meetings. Even our regional rep was not allowed to go until the last day after everything was negotiated. When they finally decided on this agreement we had three days until the vote; we were notified Thursday, and Sunday we had the meeting. They told us what was in the agreement on Friday—that all the retirees would be gone. We asked if we could have a few days to look it over and they wouldn't allow for that. We were told if we didn't vote on it that night, everybody would lose their job.

In short, they voted themselves out of work. Because management posed the outcome as an ultimatum—leave and keep the younger people working, or everybody's out—the retirees agreed to leave. Seventy of them lost their jobs. This group included Pam and two others I interviewed, Beth and Richard. None of them was over sixty years old; retirement had come too soon.

. . .

A stranger entered into Pam and Beth's lives: insecurity. Both of their husbands are older than they and already retired. Since the women's forced retirement, each couple has been living on two pensions, instead of one pension and one paycheck with benefits. Medical insurance is the biggest loss. Beth tells me this in a whisper, the consequence of a recent throat surgery; during our whole interview, I have been struggling to hear her. The bills from the operation are daunting, and she knows she won't be able to pay for her own medical coverage for long. So she is looking for a job. At fifty-eight years old, her prospects are not particularly promising. Then again, she still has a couple of decades ahead of her; subsisting on her pension isn't promising either.

Beth's pension is certainly cushioning her declining fortunes, but it is hardly the thickest of insulation. For one thing, it lacks the padding of benefits. That might be okay for those workers who have reached retirement age and can qualify for Medicare, which Beth and the others had not. For another, pensions do not adjust for inflation, and raises are out of the question—another problem for workers with long lives ahead of them. Moreover, pensions are not guaranteed; they are renegotiated with every contract agreed with younger working employees. The financial crisis made a discomfiting example of this final point. In 2008, Delphi Automotive, one of the United States' largest auto parts suppliers, declared bankruptcy. Under its reorganization, GM and the federal government were to assume responsibility for workers' pensions. More than twenty thousand workers saw up to 70 percent of their pensions slashed, and their life and health insurance disappear.[11] Yet the pensions of several thousand other Delphi employees were maintained—they happened to be members of the UAW. After all, unionized workers are 54 percent more likely than their nonunionized peers to have employer-provided pensions.[12]

An additional consequence of reduced pensions is the competition created between younger and older workers. Life expectancy has risen substantially in the last few decades, and employees can work more years before retiring. When they do so, they avoid years spent on reduced pensions, but their longer work life can become an obstacle to the employment of younger people in the market. That was exactly the dilemma faced at the Wrangler Jeep paint shop. Richard explains that his colleagues "voted to lose their jobs to keep the younger people in." To him, this pitting of the young against the old is constructed, not coincidental. Corporate management inserts wedges between groups of workers: not only younger workers against older ones but skilled trades against unskilled, first shift against second, hourly against salaried. As I researched the paint shop episode, I witnessed the acrimony myself—younger workers were unsympathetic to the plight of the retirees, condemning them on online forums as "double dippers," among other jibes. That antagonism is scary to Richard, because young people will be voting on the pensions of retired workers with each contract negotiation in the future. If they don't benefit from good pension plans, "They're not going to have a problem saying 'I have no retirement pension, screw those people that are already retired.'" Rather than uniting to close the gap between the wages of the young and old, workers are in contest over the issue.

Perhaps workers would be demanding more but for another field of contestation—that between union leaders and union members. Richard believes that "now the union is a business." George agrees. Asserting that the union has basically become "an appendage of the corporation," he contends that union leaders care more about the opinions of company managers than of the rank and file. That view might explain the exclusion of local union representatives from the paint shop negotiations recounted by Beth.

Co-opting union leadership might be a tactic in an overriding corporate strategy to weaken workers' bargaining power. Another is the shaping of public perceptions. Corporations and their political allies malign unions, reinforcing the idea that workers are responsible for the decline of the industry because they demand too much. George sums up the flawed logic of this argument: "For everything we've given in the past thirty years, since the AP Parts strike, we have given and given and given. Has the price of the vehicle come down by one nickel? No. Has the profit come up? Yes." That AP Parts strike occurred back in 1984, called by the chairman of the UAW Local 14 in Toledo. There has not been an official nationwide strike against Jeep since 1972, or one against Ford since 1976. Until 2007, GM had not faced an official nationwide strike since 1970.[13] But for occasional local or wildcat strikes, the "Big Three" have been free from strong union protestation for nearly four decades. As for his question about profits increasing, George is not speaking rhetorically. In 2010, Ford and GM reported their highest profits in more than a decade—$6.6 billion and $4.7 billion, respectively—and Chrysler reported modest gains as well.[14]

As corporate profits increase, so too do the incomes of the executives. While the industry was still recovering from the recession in 2011, Ford CEO Alan Mulally earned $28.9 million, 390 times more than his average employee; Sergio Marchionne of Chrysler earned $16.2 million; and Dan Akerson of GM earned a relatively small $9 million.[15] Meanwhile, auto industry workers make a living that seems paltry compared to that of their bosses but is significantly better than that paid workers outside the industry and the unions. In 2011, a "traditional employee"—that is, someone hired before 2007—made an average hourly wage of about $30.[16]

Let us consider that comfortable $30 per hour for a moment. The right to earn a secure middle-class income is precisely what unions fought for in the twentieth century—and it worked. In 2011, the *union wage premium* (the extra wages earned by union workers compared to nonunion workers) amounted to 13.6 percent. That is, the wages of unionized workers were 13.6 percent higher than those of their nonunion counterparts in the same industry and occupation and with similar levels of experience and education. The union wage premium also helps close the wage gap between whites and minority workers; for blacks, Hispanics, and immigrants generally, the premium ranges from 16 percent to 23 percent.[17] That's for now.

The union wage premium, as you might expect, has been decreasing in recent years. For blue-collar workers in 1978, it was twice its current rate. The decline will continue. Chrysler's new hires make around $15 per hour, about half the average wage of their older colleagues, whose comprehensive benefits they also lack.[18] Temporary employees, with even lower pay and less job security than new hires, are now kept on payrolls for durations any honest observer would label permanent.

Moreover, people have been joining unions at lower rates for decades. In Ohio, union membership reached its peak in 1989, comprising more than 20 percent of all employed wage and salary workers. In 2013, the proportion was just over 12 percent. Ohio's union membership rates have historically been just above the national average, which has declined at the same rate.[19] Among blue-collar workers specifically, the national rate of unionization in 1978 was a formidable 43 percent.[20] Today union representation varies significantly from one region to another. Table 1 illustrates the highest and lowest rates of union membership in states across the country.[21] Half of the unionized workers in the United States live in just seven states, including Ohio with its approximately 600,000 members. Union membership varies by economic sector, as well. At 35.3 percent, union membership in the public sector is substantially greater than in its private-sector percentage of 6.7, yet it is undergoing a general decline in both sectors. Age is another factor: younger workers are less likely to be union members than older ones.[22]

With corporate profits and salaries rising, union membership rates at half their peak, national strikes practically unheard of for four decades, and consistent worker concessions on benefits and wages, the autoworkers in Ohio feel unfairly maligned by the narrative blaming them for the decline in manufacturing. Meanwhile, as facilities and jobs move south—not just to Mexico but to the nonunionized southern region of these United States—conservative political movements demanding that employees have the "right to work" without paying union fees are moving north.

Still, George dreams of a union renaissance: "Either it will go 100 percent down the toilet and not exist anymore, or the people are

Table 1. Union Membership Rates, 2013

State	Percentage of Employed Belonging to Unions
With Highest Rates	
New York	25.8
Alaska	24.5
Hawaii	23.6
Washington	19.7
With Lowest Rates	
North Carolina	4.8
South Carolina	4.7
Mississippi	4.2
Arkansas	4.1

Source: U.S. Department of Labor, Bureau of Labor Statistics

going to rise up and make it a real union . . . a real organized labor union again." That dream might be folly. But for these autoworkers, the American Dream is even more fantastical. Beth had me turn my recorder back on as we were parting ways to iterate the point: "The American Dream is not there anymore, not for the young people." I turned the recorder off again; she had nothing more to say.

. . .

Working for Kenworth Truck Company in Chillicothe, Rick feels no need for a union. He's not opposed to the concept; to the contrary, "we would never be where we're at today if not for the unions." Yet Kenworth already offers him and his approximately 1,500 coworkers all the "wonderful things" the unions promised when they came in and tried to organize them. And with that, Rick is satisfied. "I work forty-five hours a week, and after thirty-eight years, I still love my job. I have been very blessed."

Besides, unions do cause some problems, according to Rick: "with wages being so high, you can't blame these companies for going outside of the United States." Kenworth has done so itself, opening a manufacturing plant in Mexico and other operations in Canada and Australia. Yet the American employees, including unionized members, remain at the main manufacturing plant in Washington State. But not all of the Ohio-based employees have been as lucky as Rick, who in his four decades as a liaison engineer for the company has only been out of work for six weeks. With 15 percent of the market share in Class 8 trucks, Kenworth felt the pain crippling the auto industry when gas prices climbed and demand fell at the start of the economic crisis. The company issued its first layoff announcement in January 2007, and then another in October; still more workers were laid off in two rounds in 2008. As recently as spring 2012, another 10 percent of Kenworth's Chillicothe workforce went home.[23] The plant's operations have at times slowed to a standstill through these years, but Kenworth kept coming back. Actually, its managers often brought back the same workers they had let go. Laying off workers only to bring them back when production picks up is an unstable arrangement at best, but Kenworth pays well and nobody's complaining too loudly.

Rick is a beneficiary of those high wages. He regards his income from Kenworth as "very fair, especially for this area." He's right: he makes about $70,000 per year in Ross County, where the median household income is $44,500. Together with his wife, who is an office manager for a small dental practice, they make a household income of about $100,000 per year. But Rick's wife only went to work in the last couple of years; previously, they were a one-income family. Actually, she took on that job because—despite the good income—Rick's family did not feel comfortable enough. Utility prices were rising faster than wages, and meeting the mortgage on his two-hundred-year-old home was never easy. Healthcare costs were also increasing (I learned later why this is a grave expense for Rick). And with gas prices high, just driving the car was taxing.

Speaking of cars, Rick was a little embarrassed to tell me about the indulgence his income has allowed him: eight cars, five of them trucks. But, as he is quick to point out, two of the pickups are basically parts vehicles for the third. At the same time, his wife's BMW sure is roadworthy. The quantity is gratuitous, but I can forgive Rick the size of his vehicles. During the SUV craze of the early 2000s, America increasingly "supersized": we expanded not just our fast food portions but portion sizes generally; embraced bling-bling pop culture; replaced houses with suburban faux chateaus; and worshipped in megachurches. Meanwhile, luxury HUMMERS (even their all-caps trade name screams "big!") roamed through our towns as fervently as the army models were trekking through Iraq and Afghanistan espousing the "you're either with us or against us" foreign policy of the times. But I'm Ohio-bred, and I know snow. In our part of the country, four-wheel drive gets a pass.

And if God is waiting to pass judgment on Rick, I suspect he also would forgive the materialism—for Rick is good. The Methodist church in town is like his home; the parishioners, like his family. He takes his "personal ministry" around town but notes that he represents only himself when doing so. About three times per week, Rick visits patients in the hospital. He makes the sick laugh with jokes too off-color to come from a church official, or he just prays by their sides. Most members of the community know Rick personally as a result, although he likes to think that the patients don't see him at all—"just the love of Christ."

Rick is deeply impressed by his Lord, who did this "awesome thing and gave us free will." And each time Rick acts in his faith, he feels the awesomeness. He did not always know God; Rick was thirty-two years old when he "finally accepted the truth"; he was home alone when the electricity went out and the Holy Spirit descended upon him. He tells me about that experience, hoping to "encourage" me. God wants a relationship with me, Rick insists. After all, "it's not really an accident for this evening to come together like it has."

I allow Rick the point; I am grateful for the evening because it did bring Rick's Lord to me. That is, it elucidated a faith-based understanding of our economic times. His divine economics goes like this: In the beginning, our country's founders proffered us a Constitution and Bill of Rights that incorporated faith. Now, "we are asking God to leave; we don't want to display the Ten Commandments, we don't want prayer in school, and we don't want Him." The consequences—i.e., the Great Recession—are rather dreadful. "We have recorded history for thousands of years, and every nation that has decided to go on its own, in denial of God, has failed." Rick's interpretation of economic cycles is not all apocalyptic gloom, however. Down here in southern Ohio, "there's a good strong base of Christian people." It may be no coincidence, then, that his company has remained relatively healthy despite the downward trends in the automotive industry.

Later that week, I recounted this conversation to a friend. When he asked how I responded to Rick's theory, I told him what I told Rick: "I used to hear the same thing when I lived in Singapore." Like Rick in Ohio, the Christians on that island-state—a large minority relative to their proportions in the surrounding Muslim and Buddhist countries of Southeast Asia—attribute Singapore's economic success to their faith. My friend expressed disappointment in me for "reinforcing" Rick's perspective. But as I learn more about Rick, about the conflicts that belie the comfortable demeanor of a man with a caravan of cars and the confidence of Christ, I find myself uninterested in secular preaching.

Rick has been twice married, once divorced. His first marriage lasted eleven years and gave him two sons; his current marriage brought him a daughter. The oldest son is a counselor at Ohio State University's hospital, pursuing a doctorate degree by night. He likes what he does—it feels good to help people. Rick is proud of him. And because his son is also good in God, Rick gets to see his granddaughter every week at church. He doesn't see the girl's mother, because his son is divorced from her. Rick's daughter from his second marriage also has a child and no spouse.

Unlike her half-brother, Rick's daughter never married in the first place. After she graduated from high school, Rick wanted her to go to college. Instead, she went to cosmetology school. Now she paints nails part-time. Meanwhile, she met a man who got her pregnant and left her. At the age of twenty-four, she moved in with her parents and had her baby. Their new granddaughter is wonderful; their daughter is challenging. "She has her ways and we have ours, and sometimes they just don't match up," Rick laments. He readily admits to the family's flaws. "I'm not comfortable with them having children and not being married," he concedes, "but that's the way it is today, whether I like it or not. I don't think it's right." Rick is generally displeased with today's youth.

I heard this repeatedly in my conversations around Ohio, so you will too: young people today just don't have the same work ethic as older generations. Cushioning his argument, Rick admits that some people his age are "worthless." The converse is true of the youth now: some are anxious to work. Yet generally, the younger generation is "really not interested in going above and doing the extra." They won't jump in and help a colleague, or do anything that might extend beyond a limited reading of their job description. Ours is a "Me, Me, Me society." As a telling example, Rick describes how one of his young coworkers ignored his morning greetings day after day; when Rick pointed this out to him, the young man barked back that he wasn't there to make friends, "just a paycheck." Worse than the attitude are the implications. If young Americans aren't inclined to work hard, corporate America is willing to export jobs. It may be worse yet: the scripture refers to the generation before the return of Christ, people who are lovers of themselves and disrespectful of authority. "I'm not saying this is the end," Rick says hesitatantly. Doom takes a seat at our table anyway.

At least Rick's eldest son is achieving in both career and school. His daughter, she has her health. That is more than can be said of the middle boy.

He loved to play baseball. Although he lived in a nearby town with his mother, the boy used to play in the league in Chillicothe to be near his dad. Then, one day in 1999 shortly after graduating from high school, he was in a car crash. He held onto his life, but traumatic brain injury degraded what remained of it. Rick reveals his agony:

> He survived, but he's not the same son. He requires assisted living. His mind is good; he has his long-term memory. And he has ambitions to go back to school, back to work. But he physically just can't do it. And people say, "Boy, you're so fortunate your son survived." And I realize that; but I don't have the same son. It doesn't matter how bad my day is, the hardest part of my day is walking into his apartment to see him. It's still challenging, after all these years. But that's something I don't want anybody to understand. It's just painful.

Rick visits his boy every day after work. From there he often continues on to the hospital, to inject hope and prayer into patients where medications fall short. Or else he goes straight home, to a house filled with the shrieks of his granddaughter, whose mother fell short. The next day he will go to work, wish his colleagues "Good morning," and smile.

. . .

Though so many engage in it, work is an intimate endeavor. Often, people spend more time at work than in school, at home, in bed, and with family. We work to make money, but our attachment to work seems to be about more than paying the bills. Our need for work is characteristic of our humanity, perhaps because it is how we seek some sense of purpose in the world. As Studs Terkel put it, work is about "a search for daily meaning as well as daily bread . . . for a sort of life rather than a Monday through Friday sort of dying."[24] When I conducted my interviews, the easy conversational transitions from work to personal life needed no prompting from me. My subjects took both pride and pain from their work lives; it was defining of their perception of self.

Yet work is also larger than each individual. A core concern in the field of economics, one that matters in all modern economies, is the *capital-labor split:* how the income from production is divided between labor and capital, that is, between wages and profit.[25] This question faces the owners and managers of multinational corporations and small businesses alike: how much of their earnings should they keep to save or invest, and how much should go to the laborers who produce the output? There is no simple economic answer to this question, no exact distribution that guarantees the success of the firm or makes everybody happy. In no small part, that's because the capital-labor split is deeply intertwined with politics.

Work is bigger than the individual and even bigger than the market. It is a political question. Naturally, capital and labor are often in contest over the distribution of income. In the past, these confrontations sometimes turned violent. The arsenal of workers is their labor power, or their collective refusal to use it; strikes are a traditional weapon of choice. Capital's strength is in its money and power, its ability to replace striking workers with "scabs," to hire private mercenaries or call in the government's police or armed forces, and to shut down operations and move production elsewhere.

George from Chrysler may be a radical by today's standards, but labor militancy worthy of the name came and went before he arrived on the shop floor. From the 1880s to the 1970s, American workers went on strike as frequently as their European counterparts. American strikes lasted longer—on average twenty days. They were also bloodier. Since 1850, more than seven hundred people, mostly workers, have been killed in strike-related violence.[26] Ohio workers have shared in these struggles, from the Great Railroad Strike of 1877 and the Great Steel Strike of 1919 to countless local strikes and individual acts of resistance.

Disputes over income distribution need not be violent or contentious. Labor and capital can and do engage in formal politics to achieve their ends. But in this realm, U.S. labor seems less successful than its European counterparts. Unlike most other advanced industrial nations, we do not have a labor party, let alone a socialist one, representing working-class interests in national politics. What gives?

Social scientists have been asking this question for a long time.[27] For some, the answer is in the nature of American ideology, capitalism, and social mobility. They point to the ability of regular people to acquire property in a country of cheap and abundant land; to the lack of feudalism in our history; and to a capitalist system in which wealth was never as concentrated as it was in the Old World. Others counter that none of these traits would prevent the emergence of class-consciousness. Rather, America's unique ethnic and racial diversity prevented the harnessing of consciousness into collective action. An especially compelling explanation—if only because it is so technical—is found in the structure of the U.S. government. With a first-past-the-post (winner-takes-all) voting system, our electoral contests are won with a simple majority; this rule correlates with a two-party system—third parties are squeezed out. Add to any of these explanations years of violent corporate and governmental repression against workers, our rivalry with the communist Soviet Union, and capital's converse success in securing its influence in national politics.

Labor's accomplishments in the workplace—in securing wages, benefits, overtime, and so forth—are more impressive than its accomplishments in national politics, whatever the historical or technical explanation. To be fair, labor has achieved a few critical goals, notably the passage of the National Labor Relations Act of 1935, which guaranteed the right to organize.[28] Yet labor's success in both realms, the workplace and national politics, has been declining for decades. I have already enumerated the significant declines in union membership. When a membership-based organization loses members, its effectiveness in representing its group interests likewise declines. In 2001, unions made up just 1 percent of organizations with representation in Washington, D.C., while corporations made up 35 percent. That latter number is rising steadily. Between 1981 and 2006, corporate representation among Washington, D.C., pressure groups increased by 62 percent; in absolute numbers, 1,898 more corporations had gained organizational representation over the course of twenty-five years. Unions, on the other hand, increased their representation by 0 percent; in absolute numbers, that's zero.[29] People keep working despite low levels of representation—they always will. But the system is not necessarily working for them.

CHAPTER THREE

Uh-oh, Now What?

March on. Do not tarry. To go forward is to move
toward perfection. March on, and fear not the
thorns, or the sharp stones on life's path.
　　—Khalil Gibran

*I work in construction. Was an ironworker by trade but about four
years ago . . . when the economy . . . everybody lost their jobs except
for a few people. They had like thirty, thirty-five employees; they only
have like five now. That was 2008. I had been with them for six years.
[Since then] I just worked for myself, tried to get jobs here and there.
Went well for a little while then a couple of years ago everything just
kind of stopped. People don't wanna spend money, scared of spending
money. I survived, but it's nothing like it was, going out to work every
day and have people waiting in line to get work done. It's not like
that anymore. Have to go out and scrape and scratch. I used to make
$17.50 an hour, probably thirty-six or thirty-eight thousand a year.
Since then, nowhere near that. Maybe twenty. I have rental properties
too, so that helps my income, helps a lot. But now people don't always
have the money when they're supposed to.*

*I have two daughters and a grandson. One is thirty-one and one
is twenty-nine. I was married for twenty-nine years. She died, had a
heart attack. That was four years ago. Yeah, that was a rough period.
. . . My oldest daughter works in Cincinnati for an insurance company*

and my other daughter goes to school for nursing and is about ready to take her state boards. Hopefully she'll get a good job. She has the child. They live with me. She was never married. It's always a strain, trying to take care of other people. Would be a lot easier if I was by myself, but that's not the way it is. Have to take care of family.

I'm not really looking for other work; I'll just work independently. If something comes along . . . but that probably won't happen. There's not a lot out there. Since my wife died, I just don't worry about it that much, you know what I mean?

—Keith, 56, Chillicothe

I wanted to know what Keith meant. But the nearly simultaneous loss of wife and job challenged my imagination. Such loss also limited expression, as Keith struggled to share his story with me. "I got to get back to work," he apologized, bringing our brief interview to an abrupt end. It happened too quickly—or I was too slow in absorbing tragedy—for me to snap a picture of him. No matter. I remember exactly his long white and blonde hair, topped with a camouflage-colored cap that cast a slight shadow over his mourning blue eyes. Though his wrinkles were deep and plentiful, not one of them took away from his good looks.

In the middle of the Great Recession, the construction industry's dependence on the floundering housing market meant that one out of five Americans in that sector was out of a job. That 20 percent unemployment rate made construction workers the downturn's biggest losers, by far. Unemployment in the manufacturing industry, the next dully drawn bar on the chart, was "just" 12 percent.[1] A graph cannot demonstrate something else Keith lost, in addition to his job and wife: his will. In its place he acquired a sense of dejection. His only gain was an adult child with a baby. Perhaps Keith was sensible in his sorrow. It isn't easy to find employment later in life; he was pushed out of the market too soon—and he knew it.

.   .   .

In her early fifties, Donna* counted herself lucky to be spared dependents (or rather, they, her). A single woman with no children, she would absorb her job loss alone. Five generations of Donna's family have lived in a rural town in Ohio, home to fewer than a thousand people. The town lies in a bucolic valley about twenty miles from a small city, where Donna's father worked in a manufacturing mill that employed many of the men in the region. Locals still refer to the company by the name it held in the twentieth century; since then, it has undergone one merger and two sales, its name changing each time. Losing value and employees with each changeover, the mill tells its own tale about the manufacturing industry in the state. When Donna was growing up, that tale was quite simple: her father worked while her mother stayed at home to raise their five children: Donna, her twin sister Debbie, and three siblings. They were middle class, "absolutely comfortable."

Times changed. As an adult, Donna, unlike her mother, would work outside the home. She passed through a few jobs after high school before settling in at Airborne Express, a package delivery company and cargo airline. The company was based in another town, Wilmington, but the long commute didn't bother Donna. She liked her job. In her fifteen years there, she worked in several different capacities, providing enough variety that the work stayed interesting. Moreover, the company treated her well, giving her good benefits, including excellent health insurance, and, in time, annual pay of nearly fifty thousand dollars. Not bad for a single woman, nor for Airborne's other eight thousand employees. At one point, according to Wilmington's mayor, one out of three households had a family member working at the air park.[2]

In 2003, the German company DHL bought Airborne and its operations in Wilmington. The layoffs would be a few years in coming, but for Donna the merger was the workers' "downfall." It was an ironic downfall, at that: "Most people worried about their jobs going overseas. In my case, overseas came here." In the wake of the 2008 economic crash, faced with losses of six million dollars per day in the United States, DHL began to lay off Airborne workers, ultimately laying off more than eight thousand people.[3] To its credit, DHL offered generous severance pay and extended health insurance to its departing employees. But short-term compensation would not put off the coming hardship. The DHL layoffs, together with other fallout from the larger economic crisis, pushed up claims for unemployment benefits in the region to their highest point in more than twenty-six years. Soon enough, the state's unemployment fund went dry and the federal government had to inject an emergency loan to Ohio of five hundred million dollars to meet demand.

A layoff never comes at a good time. But, having lost her father in October 2008, losing her job that November made it a particularly difficult period for Donna. As she put it, "They were awfully good to us, they gave us severance pays. But it doesn't make up for it; I thought I would retire there." Add to that a lawn mower blowing up and a car breaking down, and it was a "really rough six or seven months." Severance pay went toward settling her car payments, but Donna had to cut out such "luxuries" as water softener and a cell phone. For about a year, unemployment compensation helped Donna pay the bills; it also allowed her to take a break from work for a while, which admittedly felt pretty good. "But when [the unemployment compensation] was gone, it was like: 'Uh-oh, now what?'"

Just then, Donna's twin sister lost her job too. Debbie had spent sixteen years at a technology company in another small town nearby. Donna described to me the special relationship enjoyed by twins that the rest of us womb-monopolizers are not privileged enough to understand. Their bond is so tight that Debbie's husband jokes that he is married to both women. It was natural, then, for the two to tackle their troubles as a team. Luckily, the twins' brother-in-law was part-owner of a building on Main Street, and one of the retail spaces was empty. (This town's Main Street, by the way, with its single traffic light, movie-set diner, and historical theater, was charming, despite a dilapidation bordering on depression.) The twins took over the empty retail space, injected it with flair, and opened a shop that sells crafty knick-knacks and serves coffee, cookies, and whatever kind of soup and sandwiches they cook up each morning. The women work well together. They have discovered which tasks each is better at performing, and have divided the work accordingly. If for a moment they felt that running a joint business was harming their special relationship, Donna vows, they'd shutter the doors.

The shop is lovely but hardly lucrative. The crafts would appeal to tourists—if only the town ever attracted any. Some locals come in for lunch, but the diner is cheaper and the fast food more filling. The first time I entered the shop, I ordered a coffee and sat at one of two plastic folding tables. I had hoped to sit and sip as an observer for a few moments but found it exceedingly awkward: a stranger cannot hope to remain inconspicuous in such a town, let alone in a specialty shop in which one of the owners and her aunt were themselves sitting and chatting at the tables. So I told them about the woman housing me, establishing a personal connection, and then bought more cookies than I could eat, aiming for amiability. The latter wasn't necessary for my waistline or the conversation—Donna was happy to talk, and so was her aunt. Each time Donna received a phone call or a customer, her aunt prattled on to me about her personal health history; at the age of ninety, she had a lot to say. As for Donna, she repeatedly interrupted herself with raspy giggles. The ladies' demeanor lightened the discussion.

Donna explained that she and her twin Debbie are meeting their operating costs, at least. But that's because they are hardly paying any rent, thanks to their brother-in-law. For Donna, the setup is not sustainable for a single reason: health insurance. Since losing her job at Airborne, she hasn't had any. Debbie is covered by her husband's employer, but Donna has not been able to afford it on her own, and "it's scary, real scary." Except for an emergency room visit prompted by a kidney stone, she had not visited a doctor since 2008. Luckily, she's meeting the payments on those bills.

Just how much is Donna bringing in a year? She would "hate to make a guess at it." This much she knows: "It's like poverty, PAH-VER-TEE," she enunciates. She expects she can keep making her house payments—four more years to go. She's accepted lifestyle changes and "cut back on enjoyment" she used to derive from going out to the movies and restaurants and from playing the lottery. She has experienced a "rude awakening, going from having a really good job and doing whatever you want to do, whenever you want to do it, to nothing." Still, she seems prepared, or at least resigned, to accepting a simpler life—except for the lack of health insurance.

So Donna is looking for another job. Though she had put in an application for a janitorial position at the local high school a week before we met, she would probably be looking for a while. Long-term unemployment during the Great Recession averaged more than twenty-three weeks in 2010, nearly doubling the post-1945 high of twelve weeks in the early 1980s. Responding to record lengths of unemployment in 2008, the federal government extended protection through Emergency Unemployment Compensation, a federally funded program that provided additional unemployment compensation to individuals who had exhausted their state benefits. Thanks to that program, Donna received unemployment assistance for almost a year after being laid off.[4] That also put her in the 46 percent of unemployed Americans who spent *more* than twenty-six weeks out of work during this recession, the highest share in half a century.[5] Economists suggest that higher rates of long-term unemployment point to deeper structural problems in the economy not associated with shorter recessions and their more rapid recoveries. In other words, there is more keeping people out of work than the recession's immediate repercussions. The economy as a whole is weak; hence the "jobless recovery" that followed the official end of the recession. Long-term unemployment also becomes a cyclical problem for individuals—the longer they spend unemployed, the grimmer become their prospects for reemployment.

Still, Donna reminds me, "at least" she's not supporting kids too. She seems to be trying to convince herself, more than me, of the virtue of this fact. Yes, there's that.

. . .

Eric and Colleen would have liked to protect their kids from the blow of the economic crisis. Instead, they are changing their plans. Eric was born and raised in Painesville, a small city in northeastern Ohio, where the ambitiously named Grand River flows through downtown into Lake Erie. In contrast to that of the rest of the state, Painesville's population has been growing in recent decades; from 2000 to 2010, it increased by 12 percent.[6] The city's unusual growth can be attributed in part to an influx of immigrants. This is a rather unusual demographic trend for Ohio: in 2010, Hispanics accounted for 22 percent of Painesville's population, their numbers doubling in one decade and multiplying by eleven times since 1990.[7] That was far more than Ohio's overall Hispanic population of just over 3 percent, which is well below the national average. Another cause for the growth in population is the expansion of Lake Erie College, housed in the city.

Eric never went to college himself. His wife, Colleen, is only now pursuing her bachelor's degree in human resources management, with her tuition helpfully covered by her employer, the nearby Perry Nuclear Power Plant. My high school volleyball team competed in the same league as the village of Perry. We used to enter their gym fearfully, convinced that our competitors were unnaturally tall because of the effects of the power plant. Then again, my perspective may have been skewed by my own height of five foot one. Back then, I wasn't thinking about the plant as an employer, one that would lead Colleen to college.

Colleen joined Eric in Painesville, moving from Cleveland, when they married seventeen years ago. Since then, the two have become four. With their teenage son and daughter, they look the quintessential

American nuclear family, even with the tattoos running up and down the mom's and dad's arms. During our conversation, thirteen-year-old Jenna repeatedly displayed affection for her mother, hugging and nudging Colleen before losing interest in the subject matter, wandering off, and then coming back for more. Seventeen-year-old Alex was at a more standoffish age, playing it cool with his parents but nevertheless betraying his fondness for them. Eric is cool too, after all, playing as the percussionist in a heavy-metal band. I am admittedly ignorant of the genre, but it is difficult to imagine Eric harboring the inner darkness heavy metal presumably requires of its followers. His parenting is so earnest.

Eric and Colleen did not merely dream of Alex graduating from high school and continuing on to college; they had been working toward that end all their marriage. Yet when Eric lost his job, the family's diminished income came to mean that, for Alex, community college would replace university, loans would be borrowed, debt incurred. Alex would have to work part-time too. If there's a silver lining to be found—and Eric seems keen always to find one—it is that their two kids "are starting to see the value of a dollar more than they used to." Eric is counting on the outcome being the same: a college education. Colleen concedes, "It's just going to be a little bit tougher to get there." But from her perspective, the situation will only worsen by the time their daughter gets through high school. She explains that homeowners have been leaving the community and renters coming in, expanding the ranks of those opposed to the passage of a much-needed school levy. This is causing the school, in turn, to cut extracurricular activities, the very résumé fillers that help kids get into college with some scholarship funding. In short, job losses mean less money for the community as a whole and for her kids in particular. Colleen laments this "constant spiraling domino effect."

Colleen and Eric are revising their expectations downward. I repeatedly encountered the same tendency while talking to folks around Ohio. Eric and Colleen understood the process well. Eric explains some of the changes: "We were at a point where we could maybe go out to eat, go on some vacations. Now we maybe go out once every two weeks." Eric is proud that in the past he was able to take the kids on vacations to places like Disney World and Hershey Park. At least they will have memories of that, "which is really, really cool." Such treats were not within his own parents' means, especially not with six kids under their roof. Eric clearly cultivated his positive outlook early in life. As a kid, he saw a trip to the beach or the movies as "Fantastic! We watched our friends go on vacation and things like that. But my parents did the best they could."

Eric felt like he was doing his best too. Then, one day in 2006, his boss called and notified him that the industrial gas facility where he had worked for nine years would be closing, "sold overseas, just like that." While the nationwide recession began in earnest in 2007, Ohio's labor market was suffering well before that fateful downturn. Beginning in 2000, Ohio began to experience its worst job losses since the Great Depression.[8] Jobs declined from 2000 to 2003, remained stagnant from 2003 to 2006, and then declined every year from 2006 to 2010.[9] For Eric, that meant being suddenly thrown into a market that would do him few favors. Yet his struggle was not to find a job per se, but to find one with pay comparable to the one he had lost, and one suited to his particular skill set.

The first job Eric was offered had low pay and high risk factors. It was a job he would have taken before his children were in the world, but now he declined. Then he began working for a company that laid him off after only six months. He experienced temporary employment of that sort a couple of times. Other potential employers told him that they would not hire him because they could not match his previous income. He protested, "I don't really mind that; if you can give me a forty-hour-a-week job, that'd be great to start with." After two years of this precarious existence, a friend came through with a job at a machine shop. With no background or experience in machining, Eric latched on and began to learn. It was a full-time job, after all—one that makes him fifteen thousand dollars less per year than his former job in the industrial gas plant.

In the meantime, Eric and Colleen depleted her 401(k) account to compensate for Eric's lower income and watched their home's value drop by twenty thousand dollars. Again, they were not alone: more than 40 percent of adults withdrew money from their savings or retirement accounts during the recession to pay the bills. Additionally, household wealth (the net worth of a household) eroded more steeply during this recession than at any other time since World War II.[10]

Yet something less tangible than property values deflated too: hope. Colleen does not entirely lack Eric's optimism; she appreciates her own professional security. Yet she is disillusioned and somewhat fearful. In her view, the work-reward cycle has lost its credibility, and the American Dream, its promise. She grew up lacking; her parents needed welfare. So, for her, it was essential to "break that cycle, to keep working, no matter what." When she married Eric, they struggled at first. But they were also "doing" the American Dream: "work, . . . grow, . . . thrive. And then the economy kind of pulls it out from under you. . . . Our goal is basically not [to] go backwards any further. To kind of maintain, without sliding back into the system. That's what we're afraid of." She has even considered moving to Ireland, back to her roots, where the environment seems safer somehow. "I love America," she assures me, "but I just don't really like it right now."

Ireland is a questionable economic safe haven, but Colleen's disillusionment is justified. Even as a slow recovery takes hold, a return to full economic health seems improbable. During the 2012 presidential elections, Ohio's economic recovery—a tiny pace ahead of the nation's—became the poster child for competing national narratives. At that point, Ohio's unemployment rate was slightly above 7 percent, somewhat better than the 8 percent national average, and noticeably better than the 10 to 11 percent unemployment rate Ohioans had suffered in 2009 and 2010.[11] Governor John Kasich gave credit for this to his Republican Party's pro-business policies, while the Democratic president, Barack Obama, running for reelection, instead credited his decision to rescue the automotive industry, a vital organ in the state's body-economy.

As high as those unemployment rates were, they are modest compared to the "real" or "de facto" rates that incorporate broader conceptions of being out of work. The Bureau of Labor Statistics counts as unemployed those persons who do not have a job but are available and actively looking for work. Recognizing the restrictions of its own definition, the bureau itself publishes data on unemployment that takes into account "alternative measures of labor utilization," such as underemployment—that is, part-time worked performed by people who want to be working full-time. The researchers at the Center for Working-Class Studies at Youngstown State University likewise publish data on unemployment as defined more broadly, which they term the "De-Facto Unemployment Rate." Table 2 illustrates their calculations of this rate for one month during the recession, December 2009.

Table 2. De-Facto Unemployment Rate

Officially Unemployed	10%
Marginally Attached	1.5%
Discouraged	.05%
Underemployed	6%
Excess Disability	6%
Government Programs	4%
Subtotal	**27.55%**
Prison Population	1.5%
Military Population (active)	1.35%
De-Facto Unemployment Rate	**30.4%**

Source: Center for Working-Class Studies,
Youngstown State University

Note: Marginally attached and discouraged workers are the unemployed who have looked for work in the prior twelve months, but not in the prior four weeks. The underemployed are those working part-time who would like to be working full-time. Excess disability counts those persons leaving the labor force and entering into early retirement. Government programs cover those receiving government subsidies, such as the Earned Income Tax Credit, because of their low wages. The prison population is self-explanatory, although the Center for Working-Class Studies points out that the rate of incarceration has increased by 625% in the last thirty-five years. To see the whole database, visit http://cwcs.ysu.edu/resources/cwcs-projects/defacto.

In the two years that Eric struggled to find stable work, his plight would have been defined in various ways. He would have passed through official unemployment to the categories of marginal attachment and underemployment. While in the latter two, he would not have registered in official unemployment statistics. The official definition, therefore, conceals the severity of the problem. When Eric finally did land a secure job, he would have reappeared in the positive employment figures. But even there, nuances abound.

Employment figures fail to tell the story of decline in Ohio's overall labor force. Labor force participation rates account for the employed and unemployed alike. In 2011, only 64 percent of Ohioans were in the workforce. That means labor force participation in Ohio had reached its lowest rate since 1985, with male participation at its lowest point in history, and just one out of every two blacks participating.[12] Those Ohioans participating in the labor force and working are making lower wages than they used to, with the state's median wage (adjusted for inflation) falling at a rate faster than those in most of the nation. In 1979, the median wage of a worker in Ohio was $16.54 per hour; in 2011, it was $15.20. Over the last three decades, wages have declined for all income groups except for the top 20 percent. And there in those statistics we find Eric. He remained in the labor force and would be counted among those bringing down the state's unemployment rate. But he is earning less than he once could have expected to make before wages began to decline—less, in fact, than he once did.[13]

Eric and Colleen see the trends around them. But they hardly thought that their own struggle was of much concern to others. When I approached them and asked if they would talk to me about their experience of the economic crisis, a look passed between the pair. By then, I was used to couples using an unspoken language to seek approval to share personal information. With Eric and Colleen, the glance confirmed approval and then relief, soon spoken by Eric: "We have a lot to say about that."

At the close of our conversation, Eric shared one last thought with me. "That felt really good to talk about," he said. "I haven't really done that before. Thank you."

. . .

About ninety miles west of Eric's home is Huron County, where farmland is more prevalent than people and whites account for 96 percent of the population. In Norwalk, the county seat, a train runs through the city center, intermittently breaking a sleepy calm and evoking eras past. There I found Bill, seated on a bench on a sunny day. He wore cargo shorts, an orange polo shirt, and a placid demeanor. Bill was one of the first people who shared his story with me, and his approachability relaxed my nerves for the task ahead.

At first, I didn't notice the brace wrapped around his arm. Bill's disability—cerebral palsy—came into view in the course of our conversation. But in a profound sense, it remains hidden: Americans who receive disability payments are not counted in the labor force, and therefore they do not register in the ranks of the officially unemployed. But, as the researchers at Youngstown State University demonstrate in their measures of the De-Facto Unemployment Rate (table 2 above), many people receiving disability ought to be counted among the unemployed. Like Bill, their resort to government assistance is often prompted by their inability to find a job. Omitted from unemployment figures and from the labor force generally, their cases do not register in measurements of the workforce. Disability recipients constitute a growing statistical pool of people not working but not counted among the unemployed.

Bill "retired" in 2008 at the age of fifty-six, nearly a decade earlier than he had planned. That came about after he had worked for more than twenty years at the Norwalk Furniture factory. This family-owned operation, founded in 1902, became the largest employer in town, seller to nearly sixty franchise stores around the country and recipient of $163 million in sales in 2006.[14] More than a century of success, however, did not protect Norwalk Furniture from the coming economic trials.

Year after year, foreign competition increasingly threatened small and medium-sized enterprises like Norwalk, making quality products at relatively high costs. In 1992, the United States imported $129 million of furniture from China; by 2003, that figure had increased by a staggering 4,000 percent, reaching $5.28 billion. To slow the tide, the Commerce Department began imposing import tariffs on Chinese-made bedroom furniture. To bypass the tariffs, Chinese manufacturers relocated their furniture plants to other parts of the South China Sea. That shift made Vietnam the biggest source of wooden bedroom furniture sold in the United States, selling $931 million worth in 2010. Furniture workers in Vietnam make about eighty dollars per month.[15]

In the wake of the foreign furniture deluge, the domestic housing bubble burst. After increasing by 79 percent from 1997 to 2006, the value of U.S. homes began to plummet in 2007. In three years, the value of homes dropped by 33 percent.[16] The building of new homes collapsed in turn, followed by a collapse in sales for the manufacturers furnishing those homes. The owners of Norwalk Furniture needed some cash to ride out the downturn; instead, they faced the credit crunch. In July 2008, Bill and more than five hundred employees had to walk out of the Norwalk plant in Ohio, as did three hundred others at a sister plant in Mississippi.[17] The doors closed behind them.

Bill walked out with a limp. For more than two decades, he had worked for Norwalk Furniture in varying capacities: as a janitor, in maintenance, and, in the end, as an inspector. He did all this with cerebral palsy, a condition that limited his motor control in one arm and one leg. Bill was born with the disease, and his own mother aggravated the affliction by putting him down, condemning his limitations, and shaming him for his shortcomings. But Bill is proud of the jobs he performed during his career. Norwalk helped. He was unable to execute certain tasks, but "out there they were nice. They took care of handicap people, hired handicap, which was nice."

Bill is not the only person who thought fondly of Norwalk Furniture. The local community made an admirable bid to save it—and succeeded, kind of. Norwalk's mayor, along with some prominent local families (surely spurred by the county's dire 15.4 percent unemployment rate), rallied private investors and the state government for loans and support. They sought negotiations with Comerica, the bank that had refused Norwalk Furniture a line of credit. Then laid-off factory workers, with the company's sofas and chairs in tow, shuttled up to Detroit, where they protested outside of Comerica's regional office. Reporters covered the movement to save Norwalk Furniture, and the bank agreed to talk with potential buyers. Eventually, the factory reopened its doors. The rescue of Norwalk Furniture by the city of Norwalk is a touching story. But only one-tenth of the workers got their jobs back at the massively scaled-down operation.[18]

Moreover, while the furniture factory worked to reinvent itself and survive, other casualties mounted. The town's second-biggest employer, Mayflower Vehicle Systems, closed its own doors in April 2010, casting 125 more people out of work. For those suddenly out of work and looking for something else, this was not good news.

Bill was one of this pool. He was out of a job, in his late fifties, and handicapped; the market was not going to be nice to him anymore. "My savings just got down to nothing. I mean it really hurt me bad," he recollected. Bill's plight was not for want of trying. He had searched for work, "but there was just nothing out there. You know, they wouldn't hire me with one hand and one leg." So Bill applied for disability insurance. The moment he did so, his unemployment compensation stopped, once again placing him in economic danger. Scrabbling for safety, Bill dropped his cable service, cut down on groceries, and stopped drinking beer. Eventually he was awarded Social Security Disability Insurance and started receiving his monthly payments (on average, disabled workers received $13,560 per year in 2013).[19] But Bill remained deprived of something much more vital for a further year: health care. In that time, he simply did not go to the doctor. "I was just healthy enough I didn't get sick. I'm glad!" Bill chuckles as he tells me this. I giggle back, mostly at the uncomfortable irony of a man with cerebral palsy explaining how he had held off sickness for two whole years.

Eventually, through a special Medicare program for people with disabilities under sixty-five, Bill received health insurance. In a few years, the federal government will start paying him Social Security instead of Disability Insurance. At that point, Bill will no longer be hidden from the unemployment and labor force statistics; he will actually be retired.[20]

The number of Americans receiving disability payments has nearly doubled since the late 1990s. In 1998, about 4.7 million people received disability payments; by 2012, this figure had increased to 8.8 million. Although more people are applying each year, government awards of disability insurance are not keeping pace with applications; in 1998 the federal government awarded disability insurance to 52 percent of applicants; in 2012 it did so for just 35 percent. Demographic factors explain much of the increase in applications: baby boomers are coming of age, more women are participating in the labor force, and the retirement age for Social Security is rising.[21] Unemployment is another cause.

The data indicate that people resort to disability insurance when economic conditions worsen. Between 2007 and 2010, the number of applications for disability insurance received by the Social Security Administration increased by a dramatic 34 percent. (The increase from 2004 to 2007 was only 2 percent.) Over the following two years, as the economy began its slow recovery, the percentage of applicants decreased. By 2012, the number of applications was declining.[22]

This is not to say that Americans are playing the system or faking their disabilities when times get rough. There is no question that Bill's claim to disability was legitimate. But when he could work, he did. In times of economic trouble, the weaker members of our society suffer the most. Any disadvantage becomes a handicap, in all senses of the term. The disabled are more likely than other groups to experience poverty, and when they do, their impoverishment is deeper and more persistent than that of others.[23] Like Keith and Donna, Bill was pushed out of the market before his time was up. His health problems made finding another job more difficult, but they also led him to a social safety net.

.   .   .

Another kind of safety net is a partner. When Eric lost his job, Colleen's income was stretched to cover their family. The support can go both ways.

When it became clear to Susan* that her husband's family-run mail-order garden company was foundering, she went to work for Mark* in the nursery. Soon, they were shuttering the business together. Afterward, Susan secured commission-based work listing collectibles and antiques on eBay. Mark transitioned smoothly from the garden business into a new job as a financial controller for a manufacturing company south of Youngstown. Her husband's income was secure again, but Susan kept her new job. For the first time in her married life, she was contributing to the family earnings and, frankly, she was enjoying it.

Yet Susan wants to make it clear she was working before, too: she homeschooled their four children. "That was a Christian decision, more than anything else," Mark explains. Susan adds that there were a lot of reasons for choosing to homeschool. They did not want their children to be taught evolution, but they were also concerned about peer pressure, the prevalence of "broken" families in the public schools, and the quality of the teaching generally. All four of the children are now in college or graduate school, and two of them are top of their class, Susan announces proudly. Three of them are women, and I cannot help but wonder whether they will translate their education into work after graduation, or wait until hardship hits home, as their mother did.

Like Susan, Sally* had always been a stay-at-home mother. Her husband Roger* did not lose his job as an RV salesman, but with the economic downturn his commission-based income dropped apace. In 2010 and 2011, he was making about twelve thousand to fourteen thousand dollars less per year than his average annual income over his fourteen years with the company. Further, his employer stopped providing health care for Roger's family, instead covering Roger alone. To make up the difference in lost income, Roger took a part-time job at the local Walmart. Combined, the two jobs had him working sixty to eighty hours per week, and "that's just to make the bills. There's no savings account."

So Sally got a job stocking at a grocery store. This allowed Roger to quit his second job and also gave them a discount on their food. With two sons at home, that certainly helps. But it does not give them health insurance. Roger is worried about this, but for now is just "saying a lot of prayers." Sally is less concerned. "It's actually cheaper to go to the doctor without healthcare," she explains. "All you do is tell them you don't have insurance and they'll give you a discount. And you get better care, I think. Don't ask me why." I don't ask why. Sally is not the first person to tell me this.

Luckily, by 2012, RVs were selling again. While explaining the uptick, Roger revealed a genuine passion for the product. That emotion makes for a good sales pitch: "More people are finally starting to realize that camping is a nice family thing that you can do many times, versus spending two, three, four thousand dollars on a one-week trip. You can use this as an investment over and over again. Ever since nine-one-one [September 11], our business has actually thrived. It's family value." He continued on about the way camping brings relatives closer together, unlike a beach vacation; there are no bikini-clad girls for the teenage boys to chase after.

Roger holds his family values at the core of his beliefs, which extend to his active membership in a megachurch and his self-identification as a "die-hard Republican." That's also why Sally stayed home to raise the kids. Yet their twenty-four-year-old seems to have veered off the path somewhere, bouncing around from one menial job to another. At the time I spoke with his parents, he was employed part-time washing dishes. Roger admits that the boy's lack of success is "probably 'cause he didn't go to college, and he's lazy! He didn't listen to us." At least the younger one, fourteen years old, is "a good kid."

By joining their spouses in working for pay, Susan and Sally became part of the 76 percent of American married couples with two income earners in the household. It pays for both partners to work. Just a third of families with a single earner bring in more than seventy thousand dollars per year, while families with two earners account for about 85 percent of households with incomes that high. Furthermore, married women are better off than other groups of women. From 2001 to 2011, the incomes of married women rose more than those of women generally and more than those of unmarried women specifically.[24]

Men, whatever their marital status, are still more likely to live in wealthier households than their female counterparts.[25] On the other hand, the Great Recession was harder on men, who were unemployed at higher rates than women.[26] Recessions, it seems, have a strange way of balancing the genders.

. . .

Ohioans are not new to job loss. In the early 1980s, the state's official unemployment rate soared into the double digits. But back then, the decline was concentrated in particular places and sectors. This time around, Ohio and the country underwent the struggles faced by individual cities in the past, especially industrial ones, according to scholars John Russo and Sherry Lee Linkon. In their words, "Youngstown's story in the 1980s is America's story today."[27] Back then, steel towns writhed from downturns associated with deindustrialization. Other regions of the country only took notice later, when the Rust Belt's crime and corruption made headlines. Americans watched with horror as Youngstown competed with Detroit for the highest murder rate in the country.

In *Steeltown USA,* Russo and Linkon documented the consequences of economic decline in Youngstown, Ohio, the "poster child of deindustrialization." In the early twentieth century, the Youngstown area boasted the largest concentration of steel-making facilities per capita, and per square mile, in the world. By the 1970s, however, the United States was a net importer of steel, and the city's fate turned. Between 1977 and 1982 alone, five major steel mills in the area closed—thereafter, fifty thousand jobs vanished.[28] In the decades that followed, the city developed major structural problems, including depopulation, endemic crime, and pervasive corruption, that accelerated the economic deterioration. Youngstown has yet to recover from that cycle of decline.

The process of deindustrialization was strong and swift, but it did not finish the job. The people we met in the last chapter were still making cars in Toledo, a city that might have shared Youngstown's fate if not for the federal government's rescue of the automotive industry. And while Toledo was saved from the worst, people around the rest of the state did not take their non-industrial jobs for granted. In Ohio and around America, economic troubles were distributed widely.

The Great Recession was an equal opportunity unemployer. The downturn struck high-tech strongholds and middle-class professionals as well as manufacturing towns and factory workers. Whole cities were handed pink slips. Beginning in 2010, eight American communities filed for bankruptcy: San Bernardino, Mammoth Lakes, and Stockton in California; Jefferson County, Alabama; Harrisburg, Pennsylvania; Central Falls, Rhode Island; Boise County, Idaho; and Detroit, Michigan. Others, like Chicago, have teetered on the edge of insolvency, with development models unable to keep up with an impatient new economy. The fiscal crises represented by these bankruptcies could each be a marker on a long road of social and economic deterioration like that documented by Russo and Linkon.

A job loss can be highly disruptive in an individual's life. Several thousand job losses implicate society in its entirety. Russo and Linkon map the societal impact of economic decline, which originates on the individual level, goes on to affect the larger community, and can last for generations. The process looks something like this:

The social costs of deindustrialization include the loss of jobs, homes and health care; reductions in the tax base, which in turn lead to cuts in necessary services like police and fire protection; increases in crime both immediately and long-term; decaying local landscapes; increases in suicide, drug and alcohol abuse, family violence and depression; decline in nonprofits and cultural resources; and loss of faith in institutions such as government, business, unions, churches and traditional political organizations.

Take a deep breath, because the consequences might not end there. When people do find jobs again, they are likely to be paid less, receive fewer benefits, and lack job-related security.[29]

This feels like a precarious state of affairs. At the individual and societal levels, among blue- and white-collar workers alike, the modern economy seems unforgiving—for most. One can chalk it up to globalizing markets or a technological revolution; these processes certainly demand changes in the labor force. But the economy has *never* been generous to the masses. From slavery and feudal peasantry to the exploitative industrial systems of the eighteenth and nineteenth centuries, working people have lived comfortless lives for most of human history. The middle class was the great invention of the twentieth century.[30] That's when the United States inaugurated an era of social democratic transformation, beginning after the Great Depression and expanding following the Second World War. Social institutions were democratized and a social welfare state was built to bring many of the most vulnerable Americans (though less so blacks) up to a higher standard of living. For much of the century, this process served the country very well—it coincided with the years of our greatest economic growth.

It feels as if the growth and the social support are both on the decline. Might that be the fault of the globalizing market (even though it has been globalizing for more than a century)? Did Americans suddenly lose control over the processes they were once responsible for? I would suggest not. It is useful to recall that the American economy *is* still growing and remains the world's largest. But not since the Great Depression have so few people enjoyed the gains. Many are increasingly vulnerable in their jobs and comforts. When the economy dives, the losses suffered by those individuals can potentially destabilize the community around them. Individual experiences matter, but in this country, our fates are shared.

CHAPTER FOUR

Done Everything I Could

Paradise lies under the feet of mothers.
—Muhammad

I have three kids. Divorced. I'm a nurse at Mercy Cancer Center in Elyria. I've been there for like five years. I've been a nurse for a little longer than that. I switched because the money was less but the hours were more conducive to family life.

All my kids have always worked since they've been young. I taught them how to do that. I live on a budget. I'm raising them, but they get child support from their dad. And he spends time with them and helps out.

We've got thirteen acres. We rent the farmland out. It helps with the taxes a little bit. Not enough. But to sell right now would be stupid, 'cause nobody is in the market to buy something like that. No problem getting renters, farmland is very wanted around here. We have the best crops in Lorain County right now, maybe in the state. We grow corn, soybeans, wheat; it's all doing very well.

Am I middle class? Most days: days without emergencies [laughs]. The kids, they all help. They all buy their own stuff if they want anything. I was born lower-middle class. I didn't live in a box, but we certainly didn't have much. Right now, I'm part-time, making about twenty thousand. I'm also a student. I'm working on my RN at Lorain Community College. I have two more semesters and I'll be done.

I don't have healthcare. I just pay cash when I need something. The kids have healthcare through their dad. It's kind of my rebellion not to have healthcare. 'Cause, you know, you pay the insurance companies all this money and they get to decide how much you get done or not or how much you're going to pay for things. If I have to pay anyways, I can deal with my doctor. If I need something done, I call, say I don't have insurance, and they give a discount.

I think until we get some kind of financial education into the schools for these kids, to show them what it has done, there's really . . . we're going to be screwed for a long time. There's a whole generation that lived on credit that raised us. I don't live on credit, but we're cleaning up the mess. It's got to change. I'm selling the house to [my son], and when [my daughter] goes away to college, I'm planning on owning only one asset, and that's my van. I'm going to be a traveling nurse and live in my van. And I'm not going to own anything. Gotta get back to simple, you know?

—Lisa, 45, Elyria

Within six months of our first conversation, Lisa sold her home and land. Within twelve months, her ex-husband had remarried and was no longer spending much time with their kids. Such is the precarious nature of single-motherhood.

Only change is constant in Lisa's life. Changes in plans and expectations long preceded the one-year window of our meetings and correspondence. Lisa never intended to have kids. But then, she never expected to love a man so much. And the last thing she wanted was to be a nurse. "I just wanted to do every different kind of job there was and live every place there was and I didn't want to be responsible for anyone but myself." This is not to say she shoulders regret. On the contrary, her expectations for work and love were "far exceeded." She loves her kids. She loves her job. She loves that she loved.

Lisa's work life began with babysitting at the age of nine. "Kind of crazy," she admits, but back then people "were nuts," and would leave their children with an older kid. She was well trained, though:

an apprentice to her mother, who hosted an informal day care in their home. Her father, meanwhile, worked for Columbia Gas from his twenties to retirement, making just enough money for Lisa to place the family at the "lower spectrum of middle class." As soon as she turned sixteen and received her driver's license, Lisa got a job working at Pizza Hut. The hours were unstable, so she took a job at Arby's when a position opened. The Arby's schedule was better: she would get out of school at eleven o'clock, work the afternoon shift, and be home by dinnertime. But soon she learned why the store manager was eager to hire girls—he was a "pervert." Lisa wanted out, so when she graduated from high school she went up to Kelleys Island, a village on an island in Lake Erie, and tended bar. During the winter months, she attended beauty school.

Before long, Lisa met her first husband. She was twenty-two when they married, having agreed not to have children. For a couple of years, they hopped down to North Carolina and back up north, climbing mountains, whitewater rafting, and just having fun. Whenever they settled somewhere for a few months, she would cut and style hair while he found factory work. As I speak with the mature Lisa, it's not hard to imagine her younger self. With long locks of chestnut hair topped by bangs across her forehead, her youthful haircut has the effect of a curtain, opening to round cheeks, eager eyes, and a sweet smile. Later, when we talk about her current love life (or lack thereof), I tell Lisa she looks great for her age. She blushes and nods in agreement.

The protracted honeymoon took a hit when Lisa turned twenty-four and found herself pregnant. The bigger surprise was that she longed to keep the baby. "That was kind of a deal breaker," she explained. The couple divorced. "And that was cool. You know it wasn't ideal, but I understood."

Soon enough, she met Dave. This one didn't need agreements. He married Lisa and adopted her boy. Over the next fifteen years, they would have another boy and a girl and grow into their adulthood to support the kids' childhoods. For Lisa, this meant going back to school and studying to become a licensed practical nurse. Dave was getting his start in engineering.

Early on, Dave's father died. He left a large tract of land in the countryside; on it was a house—in the family for decades—that would have to be sold. Dave and Lisa had no plans for buying a home yet; "we were too young." Yet the circumstances made the young couple into homeowners. Soon thereafter, they found themselves stuck in a cycle of debt. During the 1990s, the credit card debt of the average American family increased by more than 50 percent.[1] Lisa and Dave found themselves in this pool. As soon as they paid off one expense, they fell behind on another. They used credit cards to pay off other credit cards. They began to weigh Lisa's part-time income as a nurse against the costs of gas and day care her job necessitated. In a moment of hopeful desperation, Dave proposed that they take part in a sensational program propagated by a Bible-wielding radio talk show personality from Tennessee.

Even as they enrolled in the Financial Peace University, Lisa feared the program was "just another gimmick." Dave reassured her they had nothing to lose from trying. A decade later, Lisa vows, "It was phenomenal." Just one year after buying the program's DVDs and books, their cars and motorcycle were paid off. The credit cards came next. The couple religiously followed an "envelope system" that had them cashing their paychecks and allocating a set amount of money for their expenses at the beginning of each month. Just one experience at the grocery store of dipping into an empty envelope cemented in Lisa's mind the difference between a need and a want. Dave and Lisa fixed their finances.

They had created a firm foundation for their family. In time, Dave secured a six-figure income in his field. Lisa was working part-time, dividing her compassion between her patients and her children. The family actively participated in church—Dave was on the board of trustees. And they acted on their values at home, treating each other with respect and kindness. (I heard the phrases "I love you" and "thank you" pass between Lisa and her children more times than

I could note.) Just about every chance they could, Dave and Lisa would spend time alone together. They remained in love; Dave told her so with great distress as he left her. There was another woman.

The dreams Lisa never meant to have had come true—then they ended. The whole affair was toxic. The divorce, final.

Now she lives paycheck to paycheck again, with her mother to feed and her children to shelter. She is no longer welcome in the church, shunned not by any formal measure but by the insufferable coldness of a community for whom divorce remains taboo. Her home is not hers anymore; Lisa rents a house in a neighborhood full of housewives who do not grant her a "hello." She doesn't hold it against the women; she wishes she had shielded her husband too.

After all the changes in plans and expectations, Lisa is now closer than ever before to her initial self. Her two boys have graduated high school and left the house; one is in the Navy, undergoing basic training in California, while the other lives with friends closer to Cleveland as he works at "figuring things out." That leaves the youngest child, the little girl who is her mother's closest companion. But soon she will leave too. By then, Lisa will be a registered nurse. She will sell all her assets—everything but her vintage VW van—and she will be a traveling nurse. "Gotta get back to simple."

. . .

Sandy* did not plan it this way, but with no home, no husband, no health insurance, and one car, she is living out a version of Lisa's dream. It took a lot of heartbreak and hardship to get there. She is finally, contentedly, settling down into it.

Sandy married three times and had two kids by one of her husbands. That's one less marriage than her mother, and three fewer kids by one less man. Her mother's four, "almost five," marriages did not make for as unstable a childhood as might be expected. For nineteen years, one man raised Sandy and her four siblings; he was her stepfather, but, to Sandy, he was simply her dad. He worked at a paper mill in southwest Ohio. With the blue-collar income his job provided, he took care of Sandy and her siblings as though they were his own. Stretched over a seven-person family, though, his income left Sandy's mother and stepfather "pretty strapped to raise all of us. But I don't think we ever went hungry." By the time her mother divorced the stepfather who had raised her, Sandy had already moved on to her own married life.

That first marriage was something of a hiccup. It began before Sandy graduated from high school (she still did so on time), lasted less than two years, and ended without children.

When Sandy met her second husband, she thought she had made a good catch. He worked as a railroader, then as a pipefitter. His was steady blue-collar work, like her stepfather's. Unlike Sandy, he came from relative wealth; his parents owned more than a thousand acres of land in the region. Soon after their marriage, baby Amber* joined the family. Sandy wanted another, but it took her five years to convince her husband to have a second child. By the sixth year, Sandy got her wish in the form of another girl, Brittany.* But while Sandy was still putting Brittany to her breast for milk, parenthood began to spoil. Sandy's husband picked up drinking. Worse yet, he began to gamble. Soon their money was disappearing and his relationship with his wealthy family was deteriorating. "It wasn't a priority for him to pay the rent or the utilities. There was beer in the refrigerator, but no milk. I couldn't stay there with him." When the younger daughter was two years old, Sandy got a divorce.

Moving on from that marriage would put Sandy to work. She went back to school for some secretarial classes and did a stint as an apprentice in an electrical union. Mostly, she cleaned houses, although she also tended bar a few times: "That was always a job I could get easily," she happily confides.

There was a time when Sandy's blonde hair was natural, a fair frame for eyes that are still a handsome hazel. She dresses in form-fitting feminine blouses even when she's cleaning houses. Her voice is deep so that it draws one down into her. Sandy is perhaps a little less beautiful than she once was, but she remains attractive. I'm sure this facilitated her bartending, as well as her romantic life.

But for the time being, Sandy was living without romance. Her aunt and grandmother propped her up after the second divorce, opening their homes to her. And Sandy herself was creatively frugal. With both modesty and pride, she explains to me how to make secondhand clothes look like new with a can of spray starch. In the meantime, her ex-husband was "the master of not paying child support." When the state's services found out where he was working, he quit his job before they could take any money from his paycheck. In fact, Sandy would not see any of the money he owed until her youngest daughter turned twenty-six, and then only because his parents died and the estate gave Sandy her due: twenty-eight thousand dollars.

The experience of two failed marriages did not diminish Sandy's desire for a partner. "I didn't like to be alone," she admits. "I wanted that closeness, somebody working with me to have things." Before long, Sandy married again. Just like her stepfather, her third husband worked at a mill and became guardian to her two girls. He also had two children of his own from a previous marriage. For a while they all "blended in pretty good," although they "had all the problems that next families have; his ex-wife wasn't always pleasant to me." With her girls at school, Sandy was cleaning houses around town, just like her mother.

Unfortunately, the girls did not stay in school. The eldest, Amber, quit high school just twenty-nine days before graduation. She had married at sixteen, had a baby at seventeen, and at eighteen her husband lost his patience with her juggling of education and parenting. Sandy had tried to prevent her daughter from dropping out: she had helped at the house, watched the baby, "had done everything I could." Amber quit anyway. Eventually that marriage ended, but Amber remarried and had three more children. Last year, at the age of thirty-four, she thrilled her mother with the news that she had passed the GED test and was looking at nursing schools.† "I jumped up and down . . . it's a long time coming. Mama's happy," Sandy beams.

Indeed, Sandy is confident that Amber and her four children will be okay. She considers Amber "near genius," and Amber's daughter is exhibiting smarts too. Amber is working as a home health aide, her husband is a concrete finisher, and they do well enough. They own a home.

In contrast, Sandy's younger daughter, Brittany, causes her some concern. She followed her sister's path, quitting high school during her senior year and going on to have four children. Although she never married, her children are all by the same father. Only after having the fourth child, though, is Brittany "finally seeing that [her children's father] wasn't really all that she thought he was. He's got a lot of problems. He's into drugs."

Sandy informs me that drugs, and especially prescription medications, are such a problem in this area that the local hospital had to put up a sign saying its staff won't give out any pain medicine in the emergency room. On top of her partner's drug problem, Brittany has dyslexia and simply seems to lack her older sister's professionalism. Although she, too, is working shifts as a home health aide, her income is low enough that she receives food assistance from the state. Sandy supports her daughter as she can: she's helped with rent payments, and bought Brittany a used minivan to transport all the kids around. But Sandy's help may not be necessary for long. "Brittany's seeing this new man and he's got money!" Sandy exclaims. "I'm crossing my fingers it will work out." I am left wondering if this romantic insurance policy will pay out.

That brings us back to Sandy. Nine years into her third marriage, she got another divorce. Again, she moved in with her grandmother, cleaned peoples' homes, and got by each day. Then, when her grandmother decided to live with another relative, Sandy moved in with another man.

---

† The GED, or General Educational Development test, covers five subject areas and is generally accepted as equivalent to high school credentials.

She has known this man since high school, but they did not reconnect until they were both settling divorces decades later. Fortunately, he inherited a house with some farmland from his parents. Otherwise, he's not making much money. In 2004, his employer of thirty-plus years moved operations down to Mexico. Since he was in his fifties by that time, employment prospects were slim. So he and Sandy live together in the house, with Sandy's cleaning work providing their steadiest source of income; Sandy's partner pays the taxes on the house and she splits the bills with him. She likes him and is increasingly fond of their life together. She never wanted much more than that. "There's other people living under bridges, a lot of people living a lot worse than we are. And sometimes I think, I didn't ever have a break where I got a really good high-paying job, so I'm used to not having money. And I guess that's how my life went: started out not having a lot, and ending up the same way"—so Sandy articulated the cyclical nature of her poverty.

The number of single mothers in America has been on the rise for decades. In 2010, women headed almost fifteen million U.S. households.[2] Such households constituted one-quarter of all American families that year, a far greater proportion than their 7 percent share fifty years earlier. A telling indication of the normalization of this trend is its rate of acceptance among younger generations. Whereas three-quarters of Americans over the age of fifty view the rising proportion of unmarried mothers as a significant problem, less than half of Americans between eighteen and twenty-nine years old feel the same.[3] Single-motherhood—and our reconciliation to it—is expected to continue its rise.

The poverty rates of single mothers and their children have likewise been increasing. More than half of households headed by women include children, and such households are alarmingly likely to live below the poverty line. Indeed, of families headed by women, the proportion living in poverty rose from about 33 percent in 2001 to about 41 percent by 2011, compared to about 22 percent of families headed by single fathers, and just 9 percent of married couples with children. Of the sixteen million children living in poverty in 2011, almost six in ten of them—more than nine million children—lived in families headed by women.[4] In the United States, as poor single women are begetting children, poverty is begetting poverty. At least Sandy found some comfort, at last.

. . .

Rhonda is pounding at the walls of the structure of poverty. She's lived on the east side of Cleveland all her life, apart from a stint in Columbus, when she made a brief attempt to pursue a degree at Ohio State University. Back then, she was more interested in having fun than in attending class. But having a son, Jordan, forced her to take her responsibilities more seriously. So, in her late thirties, Rhonda went back to school.

This time she went to study social work at the nearby Ursuline College. Although she received some scholarship money and financial aid, Rhonda learned the price of a private education—nearly sixty thousand dollars. Not that debt would deter her: after graduating, she immediately began studying for her master's in education at Notre Dame College to become a special education teacher (or an Intervention Specialist, in the parlance). Both of these schools are traditionally women-only colleges in Cleveland's eastern suburbs, founded by Catholic institutions. That their doors are now open to a low-income, black single mother like Rhonda surely reflects positively on the inching progress of time.

Either despite or because of the fact that Rhonda is a mother and a school social worker, she bears a conspicuous youthfulness. She is talkative and friendly and looks younger than her forty-two years. Her complexion is soft and lucent; it seems to absorb the sunlight before releasing it as a mellow glow. Her hair is done into thin, tight braids pulled back into a casual bun, displaying her double-pierced ears, the lower holes holding large silver hoop earrings. She wears a

T-shirt that participates unwittingly but fittingly in our conversation: its slogan, printed across Rhonda's chest, reads, "WHAT WILL I BE?"

A year into her master's program in education at Notre Dame, Rhonda realized what she *didn't* want to be: a teacher. So she explored switching to a master's program in applied social sciences at Case Western Reserve University, a private institution also on Cleveland's university-rich east side. She's done the calculations: it will take two and a half years to complete, and loans of more than fifty thousand dollars to pay for it. All told, Rhonda will be over one hundred thousand dollars in debt. Because she will be working in the field of social services, some of that debt will eventually be forgiven: "God, thank you. That's a blessing." Getting there is the challenge.

For now, Rhonda has a full-time job as a social worker in the Cleveland Heights-University Heights school district. Still, she feels compelled to get a part-time job too. She makes enough for her and her boy, Jordan, to get by, but Rhonda would like a little more, even if just enough to get her nails done from time to time. "Because I have a teenager," she explains, "it's not easy. It's like feeding three people." Nevertheless, their current situation is a marked improvement on that of the previous year.

During the final year of her degree program at Ursuline, Rhonda was required to intern for training hours. Unpaid. Such an internship fairly qualifies as a transparent, training-focused program rather than the kind of exploitative unpaid labor lately condemned by social critics as replacing thousands of paid positions. Nor is it supporting a plutocratic ladder of social mobility open only to those young twenty-somethings who can live off of their parents while working without pay to enhance their résumés.[5] No, this was a genuine apprenticeship for Rhonda. But that did not make it any easier.

As the internship began, Rhonda mentally prepared her son Jordan for the eight months ahead: "Listen, we're going to have to go apply for food stamps, 'cause while I'm interning I don't know how we're going to eat. Either we do that, or we don't eat." She asked him not to feel embarrassed, reminding him that his mother was indeed working hard, despite what collecting government assistance might seem to indicate. But when she went to apply for the assistance, Rhonda literally had to dress herself in confidence, donning an Ursuline College shirt, a marker of her achievement. It seemed to work: "I think they saw that and saw I was able to speak up for myself."

During those months, Rhonda's income was negligible enough to qualify her for Medicaid. Fortunately, Jordan's father took care of their son's health insurance. Still, she paid off her car and dropped their cable service, although she kept the Internet service that both she and Jordan relied on for school. She bought her groceries from three different stores, getting the best deals each offered. Nonetheless, there were days Rhonda could not be sure she would make it to her internship, afraid the car would run out of gas. One day, she admits, she lied and told them she was sick, because "I was just trying to stretch the day." As was its intent, the whole experience paid off professionally: Rhonda was offered a full-time position as a high school social worker in Cleveland Heights, a small city that forms a suburb of Cleveland.

The school exhibits some of the problems of a lower-income community, from drugs and crime to apathy and negligence, but that is not necessarily a reflection of the community itself, nor of its historical character. In the 1960s, the high school in Cleveland Heights was ranked among the top schools in Ohio; but by 2013, it ranked below 650 other schools in student performance.[6] A lot has changed, it seems. For one thing, the population of Cleveland Heights declined by more than 8 percent from 2000 to 2011 alone, while the white community shrunk by more than 13 percent in the same period.[7] School enrollment in the district, in turn, decreased by 16 percent.[8] Strikingly, although about half of Cleveland Heights's population is still white, fewer than one in five of the students in its public schools are white.[9] Many parents who can, enroll their children in private schools—and those parents are usually white.

In her position at the school, Rhonda is able to help the students who remain. She works as a liaison among guidance counselors, school administrators, teachers, and parents, to see that the kids in her program set clear educational goals and then meet them. She wants most of all to help them get to college. She is well aware that the economically disadvantaged kids have a lower chance of graduating.[10] So Rhonda tries to teach the parents how to take advantage of governmental and private resources, just as she has done in times of need. "They don't know where resources are," or how to seek them out, she explains.

But Rhonda is often disappointed in the parents. Some parents, she allows, "just do not know how to be active in their kids' education." On the other hand, "a lot of parents just choose not to and they think it's the sole responsibility of the teachers." Then she homes in: "It is really our African American males. And it's between the ages of fourteen and nineteen. The single mothers—I think they don't know how to raise the boys."

Rhonda is doing everything she can to ensure that her own boy gets an education and achieves success in life. She offers me her approach to Jordan's education and future:

I don't play. I'm very firm. I'm very stern. I told him my expectations are very high. I communicate; the teachers know me. He's too silly, but he's not disrespectful or getting in fights. I've always been active. His dad is also active. His grades are really good and I want him to go to college and hopefully not accumulate any debt. I'm thinking, "If you can get all your undergrad covered, then whatever loans you need to take out for grad school, it won't be what my debt is going to be." This fall, we're going to be working on applications and essays. I want him to make sure he gets as many scholarships as he can so that he won't have a lot of debt, because I'm still going to be paying off mine.

Just as Jordan's path is shaped by Rhonda's experience, so Rhonda's was by that of her own mother, also a single parent. By the age of sixteen, her mother already had two kids; she almost always had two jobs, as well. Young Rhonda kept busy playing sports and becoming highly involved in school, doing the things her mother "didn't have a chance to do because she chose to have her children. I think a lot of these single mothers didn't have that guidance."

Despite the endurance and determination exhibited by Rhonda and her mother, statistically speaking black single mothers and their children are highly afflicted by the cycle of poverty. The numbers pile on top of them: while 15 percent of all American women were living in poverty in 2011; the rate was 26 percent among black women, 41 percent among single mothers, and a sobering 47 percent among black single mothers—nearly one in two.

Rhonda is trying earnestly to distinguish herself from those ranks by getting educated and working. Yet although she is doing what society expects of her in order to succeed, so far she's hardly getting by. And she is not alone. According to the National Women's Law Center, "more than six hundred thousand single mothers who worked full-time year-round in 2011 lived in poverty."[11] Now that she is no longer using government assistance, Rhonda considers herself a member of the middle class. Yet she has never owned a home (though she dreams of it) and she never travels. She has never been on an airplane. She reflects, "I've never been on a vacation. Ever. I want to go to Niagara Falls. I want to go to Disney. I want to go to one of the islands. I've never been on a vacation. Ever." The line between lower and middle class is blurry indeed.

Rhonda is battling demographic trends; as yet, her victory is indeterminate. She knows what it takes to succeed and she uses every day to do work toward that goal. "I want a career," she declares, "not just a job." Unfortunately, in today's economy, a career is hardly more secure than a job. In April 2013, the Cleveland Heights school district announced forty-two new layoffs.[12]

. . .

Missy is all too familiar with school layoffs. Like Rhonda, she was a school social worker. But in 2007, the funding ran out for her position and she lost her job. Missy worked for the Paint Valley Schools, the public school district serving the kids down in the small southern town of Bainbridge. In many ways, her district is very different from Cleveland Heights. It is in a rural area in another part of the state, serving just one-sixth the students, all of them white. But both school districts share in economic disadvantage. Among the students at Paint Valley, more than one in every two is economically disadvantaged; in Cleveland Heights, two in every three students are. Both districts likewise suffer from diminishing school budgets.[13] Just ten days before Cleveland Heights announced its forty-two layoffs in April 2013, Paint Valley announced layoffs from its own staff.

At times, a governmental grant can inject vital funds into an anemic school budget. When there is additional money to be had, schools are able to pay for social workers, security guards, and other support staff. When funding is lost, those employees are lost too. That's what happened to Missy. In 2000, Paint Valley used grant money to open up new positions. The district hired Missy as a social worker. Having served her community since college, Missy was a most suitable candidate: she had worked at a foster care agency, an alcohol and drug agency, and shortly before being hired into the Paint Valley Schools, at a mental health center. She happily made the career move into the schools as a social worker; her sons were at Paint Valley and she liked the idea of serving the district's youth. But by 2007, the grant money had run out. The school district couldn't afford to pay her salary, and Missy was laid off.

The impact of support staff on any school's well-being is not easily quantifiable. Since the implementation of No Child Left Behind under President George W. Bush, schools have been stringently testing for reading and mathematics skills to meet government standards. If certain methods or even teachers do not raise scores, that weakness can be targeted for improvement or elimination. But it is hard to quantify the impact of social work in improving the emotional focus or mental health of a student at a set moment in time, and harder yet to measure how critical that improvement is to a student's test scores, the government's markers of school health. Under current funding structures, these support staff are vulnerable when economic times are tight. One thinking outside the prevailing logic might conclude that it is precisely during those times—when financial insecurity renders home life precarious—that the work of social workers like Missy is especially critical.

Indeed, Missy suspects that the many problems she dealt with have only worsened since the Great Recession. She lists the issues for me: "the number of kids who have lost parents to death, a lot of poverty, basic needs just don't get met. . . . A lot of kids whose families have lost housing and they live with whoever; they're kind of like the hidden homeless: they have no home of their own but they have a roof over their head." That last point about "the hidden homeless" was corroborated by the director of a food pantry in Bainbridge, who told me, "Our biggest family is of ten right now, four generations under one roof. And we're seeing more and more of that, reporting of kids moving back home, parents moving in; and it's always a financial reason."

Missy is more concerned about the effect of layoffs like hers on the students than on herself. "Since 2007," she informs me, "our un-excused absences have increased significantly; our graduation rate has decreased; the kids are just not getting served." The district's four-year graduation rate did in fact decline by more than three percentage points between 2007 and 2012. Yet by the standards of the Ohio Department of Education, the school has actually improved its standing in the system. It is no longer designated as "at risk," as it was in 2008. Ohio's schools are "graded" primarily on the basis of assessment tests for mathematics and reading (with other core subjects assessed intermittently), in addition to attendance and graduation rates. For a district to "earn an indicator of achievement," 75 percent of its students must pass the assessment tests. Within the context of standardized testing, this strikes me as a pretty low bar for achievement. Under this system, one out of four students will not pass mathematics and reading tests and will continue to float up through the system until the next test. What is going on in the home of that student? Who is paying attention to her at school? Not Missy, anymore.

Net improvement in the school's performance, whether or not by official standards, is surely important. But Missy's perception is valuable because it reflects community attitudes about the school system—attitudes with consequences. Nobody in town was bragging about the merits of a Paint Valley education. Most people I spoke with doubted that the school was doing much of anything for the younger generations. And, in fact, one statistic speaks unequivocally to the issue of how well students are being served: over just one decade, from 2000 to 2010, the population of the city of Bainbridge declined by 15 percent. With no opportunities at home, people leave. As the population declines, so do the school's enrollment and its budget. And the cycle reinforces itself.

Unlike Rhonda and Sandy, Missy is a married mother. So when she lost her job, her husband's income continued to support the household. But not for long. In January 2009, he too lost his job as the manager of a sawmill. He was already more than fifty-five years old. Like other people in these pages pushed out before their time, he did not have high hopes of finding employment. Missy was under no illusions: "Physically, his back is real bad. He's overweight. What could he do at that age? He's lost some teeth. Who'd hire him?" Thankfully, Missy had inherited farmland from her father in 2006, and they both put their efforts into eking out some income from it. Then, in 2011, Missy got a new job. Just as in her past positions, her work would be dedicated to serving others. This time, she would be a coordinator for elderly Masons through the Ohio Masonic Home, providing for "members of the community who need assistance to stay in their homes."

Like Rhonda and Sandy, Missy is now her family's breadwinner. As a married mother, she is the "primary provider" for her household, whereas Rhonda and Sandy, as single mothers, are the "sole providers." Together, these two categories of female breadwinners now account for a record 40 percent of all American households, up from just 11 percent in 1960.[14] Of these female breadwinners, more than five million are married mothers. There are important differences between the primary and sole providers, the married mothers and their single counterparts. Like Missy, married mother providers tend to be white, well educated, and middle-aged. They also bring in more money than the unmarried mothers. Households with female primary providers had a median income of eighty thousand dollars in 2011, versus a median income of just twenty-three thousand dollars for single-mother households. Two critical developments have allowed mothers to increase their income so much that many of them out-earn their husbands: work and education. In 1968, just 37 percent of married women with children were in the labor force; in 2011, 65 percent of them were in the workplace. Within most couples, spouses attain similar education levels. Yet today, nearly a quarter of women are more educated than their husbands, versus just 7 percent of women in 1960.[15] Missy and her husband both have bachelors' degrees (they met in college); but while her husband wore a blue collar to work, she donned white. When both lost their jobs, Missy was reemployed and became the primary breadwinner.

Indeed, Missy had been on the path to more education. She had loved her job at Paint Valley so much that she wanted to take it to the next level, so she had enrolled in a graduate program to study school psychology. She was in the middle of her degree when Paint Valley laid her off. Without the income to pay the tuition, she quit. Why? "I didn't want to go into debt for my own master's degree," she explains, "because I had two kids coming up who I needed to keep my credit open to get them through college." She continues, "So, being laid off from Paint Valley just about did me in. It really was a tough one. That position just doesn't exist anymore and it breaks my heart." Even after the layoff, Missy wanted to remain involved; she now serves on the school board.

When a phone call interrupts our conversation, I learn that Missy is also an active member of the women's group at church. The caller was the director of the local food pantry. Like churches across the country that support food pantries, shelters, and soup kitchens, Missy's congregation aids the pantry in Bainbridge. But the purpose of this call was to discuss the agenda of the upcoming women's group meeting at church. When Missy hangs up the phone, she apologizes for the disruption and smiles. It is the smile of a caregiver. If you are older, you have probably seen it on your librarian or schoolteacher. If you are younger, you've probably also seen it on your doctor or professor. Women possess that smile uniquely, conveying at once their strength and their tenderness.

· · ·

The women in these pages embody the advancements of our time. Feminists of the twentieth century battled institutions of patriarchy that were millennia in the making. Now women in Ohio and around the world are attaining the education and work opportunities our forebears struggled for. In fact, as they are excelling on that road, men seem to be stagnating. In America, where women have entered the labor force in record numbers, men are falling out of it at higher rates than ever before. During the recession, men suffered more un-employment than women. Around the world, women are attaining higher academic degrees and at higher rates than men. Equality is not manifest, not at all. Men still make more money, dominate in politics, and hold the highest posts in business and finance. But the pace of women's advancement is remarkable.

Yet problems have accompanied progress. With more opportunities than ever, women are overburdened because their responsibilities as wives and mothers have not lessened. Women are now expected to perform productive *and* reproductive labor—and find time to sleep if they are lucky. In the terms of today's debates, women are struggling to "have it all." That is, they are challenged to attain professional, familial, and personal fulfillment in an age of access to opportunities that have come on top of, rather than in place of, traditional gender roles. A lively discussion has ensued, with some high-achieving women declaring the effort futile and returning home to raise their children.[16] Other women have expressed that returning home is equally unsatisfactory and are "opting back in" to the workplace.[17]

Frustrating as it is, the conundrum of balancing work and mothering is a marker of women's progress. Even so, I had dismissed the issue as irrelevant to the women in this chapter and elsewhere. I had assumed that for working-class women this debate is a privilege; they do not have the luxury of reflecting on the satisfaction they derive from work. A woman like Rhonda, I had thought, has little choice but to raise Jordan and to work. But then I thought again, and came to believe that my defense of working-class women was misguided, if well-intentioned.

Rhonda wasn't working and making money to raise Jordan—she was acquiring debt and going to school to fulfill her own ambitions. Likewise, Lisa was working as a nurse only part-time, while also going to school and harboring the goal of winning free of financial obligations in the future. Sandy, with two girls followed by eight grandchildren and no stable income-earning partner, contentedly settled into arrangements that did not reward her with secure earnings. All of these women supported their children, but none of them were placing work and income above all else to do so. These women can and do choose between family and work. It turns out that they do not always choose work.

In an analysis of women in New York City, sociologist Sarah Damaske asks how class and gender shape women's decisions to work or stay at home to raise their families. Damaske's conclusions corroborated my observations. To begin with, middle-class women, precisely because of their higher educational attainment, expect to work continually (that is, even after having children) more often than do working-class women.[18] And more often than not, they do just that. In contrast, because their jobs are often low paying or low status, working-class women perceive their work as less crucial to the household income. Many of these working-class women do find satisfying work; often, they remain in the workforce despite having lower initial expectations than their middle-class peers of doing so. But when work conditions are unsatisfying, they are more easily convinced to return home. These related trends would indicate that their work decisions are based on satisfaction and expectations, not fundamentally on financial necessity.

Through Damaske, I was liberated of the misconception that the lives of these women, because they are economically insecure, are also economically determined. Their decisions take into account personal desires as well as the state of their bank balances: there is some liberation to be had after all. Unfortunately, government policies can take little credit for that.

As American women enter into the labor force in record numbers, the government seems to have altogether overlooked their arrival. Among thirty-eight rich, industrialized nations, only one does not guarantee paid maternity leave—the United States, which offers just twelve weeks of "protected leave" (read: unpaid) instead. German women, meanwhile, are guaranteed fourteen weeks of paid maternity leave; French women, sixteen weeks; Irish women, twenty-six weeks; and British women, thirty-nine weeks. And American women? They are guaranteed zero weeks of paid leave.[19] One would hope that we at least fare better compared with women in poorer nations—but we don't. From Brazil to Burkina Faso, 97 percent of 167 countries provide at least some cash benefits during maternity leave. The United States is one of only 5 countries failing to do so.[20]

The U.S. system relies instead on employers, and in some cases state governments, to provide leave. Since 1993, the Family Medical

Leave Act has mandated that employers allow up to twelve weeks of *unpaid* leave for medical reasons—although that does not apply to companies with fewer than fifty employees. Employers decide whether to pay mothers during their leave, and practices vary. While about half of working mothers receive some pay during maternity leave, just 16 percent of companies offered fully paid maternity leave in 2008.[21]

Maternal leave is not the only area in which we lag behind. Many of the world's children—and their working mothers—benefit from preschool. The United States, however, ranked behind twenty-three other rich countries in the preschool participation rate of three-year-olds in 2012. We also followed behind twenty other countries in the extent of our government's investment in early childhood education.[22] The benefits of preschool for later educational achievement, and of maternity leave for family well-being, are widely acknowledged. Yet in this policy context, the question of whether women can "have it all" is merely rhetorical.

CHAPTER FIVE

Sweating through Your Boots

Have always in view not only the present but also the coming generations, even those whose faces are yet beneath the surface of the ground—the unborn of the future Nation.

—The Constitution of the Iroquois Nations

I'm from Cleveland, Ohio. East side, mostly—East Cleveland. Moved around a lot, at least about probably three or four years apart at a time. Maybe [because of] the areas, the foundation, the people . . . pretty much try to find somewhere decent where you can relax, have no problems.

I rap for real, but I just haven't made it a big thing. But I rap. Right now I'm workin' at a hotel. They put me on different positions. I might do housekeeping, laundry, dishes. I'm like a fill-in. Been there about four, five months. Before, I actually wasn't doing nothin', really. I was just chilling, for real. I was just trying to go to school, but it wasn't workin' out for me. Actually, I didn't even make it to high school; I stopped goin' in like tenth grade. I stopped. I was a kid, I didn't know better, didn't know how big stuff is, how important it is to have. If I could change it I would.

My father was around, I knew where he was and all, he visited, I seen him. But it was mostly my mom, I lived with my mom most of the time. It was just me, her, and I got two younger sisters. We all got different daddies.

I'm young, so when I started workin', it wasn't really that bad. Now I'm gettin' older, it's changing. It's weird, it's like, I never really had a good run on my own. My mom, she did the best she could. On her end, she kept a roof over our head, kept clothes on our backs. You know, she's dean's list, she's a paralegal. She graduated high school even when she was pregnant with me, so she never stopped. She went got her degree for paralegal. I think it's a bachelor's. She caught up, I don't know how. She's been comin' along. I just haven't.

There's a lot of people around me, I'd say 35 percent out of a hundred, don't have jobs, I would say. Actually, more than that, maybe 65 or 70 percent don't have jobs. It could be better. It could definitely be better.

I get assistance; I get food stamps, once a month. It would be nice to get married, to have a real family and stuff, I would like that. Probably, it's probably crazy, for real, I'd say I make between seven hundred and a thousand a month. I live with my mom. My sisters doin' good too, I'm the only one tryin' to get it back together. They both got their own spots. They both have kids. They have a boy apiece. No, they're not married. But their baby-daddies watch the kids. It's a little ghetto, I guess [laughs].

—Darnell, 26, Cleveland

While speaking to Darnell,* my thoughts were with his mother. She had had three children from as many men, but it seemed she was making a decent present out of a challenging past. By pursuing her education and career while repeatedly moving the family in search of safer neighborhoods, she was trying to stay one step ahead of poverty. She "caught up," in Darnell's words.

Her son has not caught up, and it seems unlikely that he will. Instead, he has slipped into a cycle of poverty that will tighten its grip on him—young, black, male—and probably not lose its hold.

Born into it, Darnell sealed the cycle the day he dropped out of high school. Of young blacks his age, 14 percent dropped out of high school when they were teenagers, double the percentage of whites of the same age.[1] He spent the subsequent years floating between menial part-time jobs and no work at all—aside from making rap music. In those same years, employment among blacks his age who lacked a high school diploma was only 40 percent, compared to a rate of 70 percent employment among all people in his age group. When those young blacks without a high school diploma *are* working, they are employed for short periods of time, shorter even than the periods worked by whites who also dropped out. The racial gap in employment is much narrower among youths who have earned at least a bachelor's degree. Young blacks with a bachelor's degree or more are employed almost as much as their white counterparts.[2] As the members of Darnell's age cohort grow older, those with less education will fare poorly; the blacks among them will fare worse.

The cycle of poverty might be nebulous but it is real. Darnell is a case in point. His race, limited education, family structure, unstable residence, and precarious work history are all linked. Born in an impoverished neighborhood, Darnell attended a substandard public school system insufficiently funded by taxes on down-market property—the school failed to retain him. Moreover, neuroscientists have consistently found that socioeconomic status is linked to childhood brain development—that is, poverty hurts babies' brains.[3] Darnell's choices matter, but an enormous structure buttressed by systemic inequality of opportunity stood up against him from the day he was born to a poor black single mother in America.

Still, some individuals overcome the cycle. For all the distressing statistics, there are corresponding numbers that round out the 100 percent. Ariana is one of the people who beat the odds.

Ariana is black, in her midtwenties, and from a similarly depressed part of Cleveland to that where Darnell grew up. Ariana's parents have been together all her life. As for her relationship status, "My school and work is my relationship," she says. And so the paths taken by Ariana and Darnell diverged.

Ariana attends Cleveland State University full time, studying public relations. She also has a full-time job as a bank teller. As if those two commitments were not enough, she does event planning on the side for the community. Rather than exhaustion, Ariana expresses enthusiasm as she explains this to me. "I work during the day and at night I'm at school. I love it though. I have been doing that for three years. I'm loving it." When she completes her bachelor's degree, she wants to stop working at the bank and formally start her own event-planning company. Not only that, but "I'm going to get my master's degree when I'm done. I'm not stopping!" she declares, beaming.

If she does go on to pursue a graduate degree, Ariana concedes, she will "probably be in debt for the rest of [her] life." Her extraordinary debt will place Ariana among the most ordinary students in our country. In 1992, fewer than five in ten students graduated college with debt. By 2012, more than seven out of ten students had borrowed money to pay for college, each owing, on average, about thirty thousand dollars.[4] By 2013, altogether, student debt stood at $1.2 trillion, the second-largest source of consumer debt in America, just behind mortgages.[5] This was the only consumer debt pool to grow after the recession.

I spoke to many middle-aged Americans who paid for their education through a combination of part-time work and family assistance. Yet for most youth seeking higher education today, paying out of pocket is just not possible. Between 1990 and 2008, the median household income rose by 20 percent. Over that same period, the cost of attending a four-year public college rose by 60 percent, and that of attending a four-year private college by 43 percent (figures adjusted for inflation).[6] Tuition rates have risen, in part, because of declines in government funding for schools. Colleges have adjusted to cuts by passing the cost on to students.† In 1985, colleges relied on tuition for 23 percent of their operating expenses; in 2010 that figure had risen to 40 percent.[7] Hence debt.

It is risky for people who have yet to establish their financial security (a characteristic quite inherent to students) to take on large amounts of debt. Indeed, two out of five students who borrow to finance their education are delinquent within the first five years

†A large proportion of students do not pay the "sticker price" of tuition, which is frequently offset by financial aid and grants. That was also the case in the past. Since the 1970s, though, the sticker price and the actual cost have risen together.

of repayment.[8] More than five million borrowers have at least one student loan account that is past due.[9] Some speculate that college debt will be the next bubble to burst and damage the economy. Even if we do not reach such a severe crescendo, the expanding debt is smothering young adults.

When more debt combines with an economic slump, young people struggle to move toward other milestones of adulthood, such as buying a home, which also requires borrowing. Whereas first-time home buyers typically accounted for 40 percent of total buyers in the early 2000s, that proportion had declined by almost ten points by 2011 and 2012. Potential first-time home buyers were deterred by student debt and other factors working against them, including the difficulty of securing mortgage financing in the wake of the housing crisis and the purchases of lower-priced properties by investors (who often paid with cash).[10] Indeed, almost half of young people delayed purchasing a home during the slump.[11]

Ariana is not considering buying a home yet, but she would like at least to rent her own place. Once she is done with school, she is thinking about moving down to Columbus. With her event-planning skills in tow, she sees such a move as a chance to "help out another city." Apparently, Ariana feels indebted in more ways than one.

.   .   .

While Ariana is seeking to move out, Stephanie* is just settling back in with her parents. The transition hasn't been easy.

Her environs are perfectly pleasant. The family home, passed through generations, is a few minutes' drive from the town center—marked by its two traffic lights—in rural Ohio. The house is also a short walk from the public school Stephanie attended, a school in which most of the students, like Stephanie, are white. When they were younger, Stephanie and her brother could go home for lunch and be back in time for class. Their father made his living in education, their mother in health care. On weekends, the family attended church together. Stephanie counted the members of the youth group as her best friends; she led worship for them before taking off to college.

The move from small town high school to small town college was eased by her faith. Stephanie sought out a church community, and assumed a role in it. As before, this helped shield her from the social problems around her. She knew that kids were smoking cigarettes in the bathroom in high school and that a lot of college kids indulged in alcohol. "There were probably drugs around, but I never really realized it, I guess." Not until her college graduation did she become fully aware that drug abuse was "all over the place. Pills was the main thing, probably also crack and cocaine. Some houses got busted—or exploded—for meth."

Stephanie stood out from many of her peers who were afflicted by the social ills of economically struggling rural areas. Struck by this during our first interview, I inquired about her sex life—not my norm. While "a lot" of her friends had had babies outside of marriage, she told me, nobody had interested her yet. I asked whether her abstinence was related to her faith. She said no: "It was more just my parents. I never wanted to disappoint my parents." I noticed her reddening slightly under the knit cap that covered her tied-back hair. Makeup was not causing the effect—Stephanie did not wear it. To do so would have looked odd on a young woman wearing a tie-dye T-shirt and baggy gym pants. I ceased my probing.

Stephanie had not originally planned to return home after college, but her parents were supportive and she had few options. By the time she graduated, her chosen major had lost its appeal: "I don't know if I was just burnt out from it or what," she said. The one thing she remained sure of was her trust in God. But however fervent, her faith was unlikely to undo the four years spent getting an education she wouldn't use. Of course, Stephanie might not have found many jobs available in that field anyway; the Great Recession was in full force when she received her diploma.

Upon arriving home, Stephanie found a part-time job in social care, assisting handicapped individuals. I'm reminded of her mother and father's careers, realizing that the whole family works in social and public service. She tells me about the job: "It's like a big family, that's a big plus. But it is stressful because some of them have behaviors that are hard to deal with sometimes, but you just do and show them the love like you would if they didn't have behaviors." Stephanie may have loved her clients, but she was not enamored of part-time work.

Stephanie's circumstances are all too common for young people in the labor market. Underemployment comes in two forms: the part-time employment of people who want to be working full-time, and employment of college graduates in jobs that do not require a college degree. Underemployment afflicts young age groups at the highest rates. In 2011, more than a quarter of eighteen- to twenty-year-olds were underemployed, as were 16 percent of twenty-five- to thirty-four-year-olds.[12] More than half of young people wanted to be working more and earning more.[13] Despite such rocky beginnings, economists point out that eventually the young and underemployed will find college-level jobs—probably by their thirties.[14] But for those graduating into a recession, like Stephanie, the beginnings are even rockier.

Stephanie was getting by on the low pay because she lived with her parents. Many young people likewise "boomeranged" home during the recession, or never left in the first place. In 2010, more than half of eighteen- to twenty-four-year-olds lived with their parents.[15] A few years later, living at home was still common for new and less recent graduates alike. Some observers have come to believe that by returning home, members of the "boomerang generation" are making more deliberate and far-sighted financial decisions than they are typically given credit for.[16] Sticking around the parental home may also help explain another development among younger generations: they are starting their own families a little later. Whereas in 1975, men were, on average, twenty-three years old and women twenty-one years old when they married, today, men average twenty-nine years of age and women, twenty-seven.[17] In turn, they are having children later too.[18]

Her living expenses were covered, but Stephanie remained financially challenged. Her most immediate concern was health insurance, or a pending lack thereof. She noted that "Obamacare has been good for me," allowing her to remain on her mother's health insurance plan until the age of twenty-six. But that deadline was coming up, and Stephanie was dreading dealing with it. More than likely, she would learn a lesson about high premiums.

Dissatisfaction with her job and the need for personal fulfillment were of equal concern. So she resolved to earn a master's degree in religious studies. That field was a world away from her first degree but much closer to her heart. Specifically, she planned to attend Liberty University, the "largest private non-profit university in the nation . . . and the largest Christian university in the world."[19] Founded by the Southern Baptist televangelist Jerry Falwell, Liberty offers online programs that would have allowed Stephanie to study from home and continue working part-time.

Yet when I followed up with her six months later, I learned that Liberty was no longer an option; the school had decided that she lacked the required prerequisites, despite her years of service to the church. Twelve months later, Stephanie informed me that her life had "flipped completely."

Stephanie had met someone. Her new friend—that's all it was at first—was a churchgoer who worked with children; their bond had grown easily out of their similarities. Both were also in transitional and uncertain phases in their lives. The support they provided each other deepened into affection. Romance ensued.

But there was a problem. Stephanie's new partner was, technically, married. While the divorce was still in process, the couple had separated, moved out, and settled on a routine to share their three children. Yet in the eyes of the church, her friend was still married and was engaged in an extramarital affair with Stephanie—at least that is the transgression the church addressed explicitly.

The unraveling began when a member of the congregation had discovered the illicit relationship and spread the word. Soon Stephanie's parents found out; seeking guidance, they told the church pastor. The pastor summoned Stephanie to discuss her sins. Stating that the relationship was unacceptable, he insisted that it could not go on. All the while, he had successfully managed to leave unspoken the offense that was shattering her parents and stirring the churchgoers: Stephanie's partner was a woman.

At home, nothing was left unsaid. Her parents, astonished at the revelation, were "completely wrecked." How did they end up with a gay child, after all the faith they had instilled in her? What wrong had they done in the course of their humble lives? They were not alone in their struggle to reconcile their long-held values with this new reality. Stephanie too asked herself these questions. She had been attracted to women in the past, yes. But not until this particular woman entered her life had she even imagined pursuing such feelings. Indeed, she has yet to grapple with her "sexuality" as such. Whether she is a lesbian or bisexual is unclear, and maybe unimportant. All she knows is this relationship, and that she wants to retain it.

With the passage of some time, things became less "crappy" at home. The love Stephanie's parents have for their daughter—and hers for them—has allowed for some acceptance. It probably helps that they witness her joy. In her relationship with her girlfriend, Stephanie is "happier than I've ever been in my life." Moreover, she finally landed a full-time job, one that came with a solid base salary, benefits, and a retirement plan. The work is a world away from religious studies. She has not lost her faith, but she has found a more accepting church to attend with her partner in a nearby city.

The future still holds uncertainty—perhaps as much as ever. The couple does not know how they will live together. They "worry about persecution," and especially about the reactions of their employers. They are fearful about coming out to the community, which lacks her parents' capacity for unconditional love. But for today, life is good—like Stephanie.

· · ·

Sarah* had planned to live with her parents during college to offset the costs of attendance. But that plan had been formulated when her parents still had a home. So Sarah found another way to afford school: she joined the United States Army Reserve. She received her education, and became a leader to boot.

I regret that I cannot name the location of the reserve unit in which Sarah serves. I will say this: industrial landscapes possess a particular beauty, one akin to a fading star. The grand towers of steel and concrete stand testament to humankind's unique ability to build a world atop that given to us. The manufacturing plants near Sarah's unit line a river filled with ships transporting goods along a waterway that leads to all corners of the globe. Despite the environmental sensibilities they offended in their prime, the dependence on fossil fuels they perpetuated, the workers that have suffered inside their walls, these plants once produced output critical to the country's energy, employment, and economy; now, their tall stacks emit primarily nostalgia. Machines are rendering their remaining workers insignificant. That's why many of the locals have joined the local arm of the U.S. Army Reserve.

Unlike most of these reservists, Sarah was driven to the unit by something entirely different than deindustrialization. Her journey from another part of the state had been unexpected. When she graduated from high school in 2003, Sarah enrolled in community college. She had calculated that if she delivered pizza full-time and lived at home with her mother and stepfather, she could afford tuition without having to incur debt. But one morning, just three weeks into her first semester, that security fell out from under her. Sarah's mother had jolted her awake: "The truck's out front—we're moving out," she cried. Sarah's stepfather, it turned out, had not been paying the rent.

The family moved into a hotel for one month. Then each of them found a separate place to go. For Sarah, that was a coworker's apartment. She still attended school; they both delivered pizza. But in those close quarters she learned of his vices: just three weeks after she moved in with him, he died of a heroin overdose. Fortunately, another friend offered her a room for an affordable price. She moved in and managed to get by for eight months, exhausted and driven to drink at the end of each long day of school and work. Her earnings spent almost entirely on tuition, Sarah was grateful not to be accumulating debt but frustrated not to be saving any money either. Enter a helping hand, in the form of a recruiter for the U.S. Army. Sarah just needed a step up to continue her education, "not a total rescue and a whole new life." That's why she chose the army reserve instead of active duty. The reserve's benefits were ideal for her purposes: she could go to school full-time and "not take ten years to get a degree done" as she worried might have been the case on active duty. She took the army's entrance exam and scored an impressive ninety-one out of one hundred. An opening appeared at a unit on the other side of Ohio—not far from a state university—and the benefits bellowed forth: an $8,000 enlistment bonus, a $20,000 student loan repayment plan, tuition assistance for some courses, a $350 per month "kicker," and a commensurate amount per month from the GI Bill. Sarah had secured her schooling.

The girl who had once dreamed of being a dentist now found herself playing the role of a soldier, "one weekend a month, two weeks a year," in the army reserve. After basic training, she settled into her new environment at school. Just two weeks into the first semester, Sarah received another jolt from her mother: "Your stepfather died." This time, at least, Sarah was safe from the fallout.

Through the army reserve, she had created a safety net for herself, but initially she struggled to fit into it. The gender imbalance was the first point of discomfort. Of all enlisted soldiers in the U.S. military in 2012, only 14 percent were women.[20] That proportion is low, but still higher than the proportion Sarah encountered during basic combat training, her first immersion in the reserve. During that period, her company was matched with a company of combat engineers who are, by mandate, men only. Thus, Sarah found herself one of only eight women in a group of about two hundred soldiers.

By the end of training, three women had quit; Sarah and four others remained.

Despite her performance on the entry exam (and because of her location preferences), Sarah was trained in a military occupational specialty that required relatively low qualifying scores and high physical demand. Men in her unit outnumbered women twelve to one.† If we could quantify excess masculinity, the proportions would be skewed further still. In a candid moment, she speaks plainly about her company: "You have a bunch of stupid people who all they care about is their brute strength." So, she added, "they were really pissed off that I got assigned to them."

At her first annual training, one of the men made a point of demonstrating just how pissed off he was. During a lunch break, Sarah's section sergeant "smoked" a few of the soldiers, commanding them to do push-ups. After a few minutes, he allowed the three men to recover, requiring Sarah to continue her push-ups alone. Eventually the sergeant came down to her level, kneeling in until his face was a few inches away from hers.

"I'm going to push you so hard to make you quit," he spit.

"Why, Sergeant? Do you think I can be a better soldier than I am?" Sarah asked.

"No, because I don't want you here. Women don't belong here."

Without permission to recover, Sarah stopped her push-ups, stood on her feet, and walked away.

That sergeant was second in her chain of command, so Sarah expressed her dismay at the incident to her squad leader, first in the chain of command. His response stung: "I agree with him, women

---

†Some military occupation specialties are more gender-balanced than Sarah's, which I am not naming in order to protect her identity. Others, like the combat engineers mentioned, are not open to women at all.

don't belong in the army." In front of the gathering crew of men, he continued, "The only purpose that women have is to be nurses or to make the men happy." For some of Sarah's fellow soldiers, the sexism of their superiors served as an example suitable for replication. In one instance, several men gathered around and challenged her ability to contribute "as much as him," referring to an enormous bodybuilding soldier passing by at that moment. Sarah is smart. She turned the question right back around on them.

She also insisted that her abilities were complementary to theirs, even if not always identical. Not only did Sarah have a role as a team member, but she wanted to become a leader as well. The challenges posed by her superior gave her just the motivation she needed. "He was such a horrible leader that he made me become better," she explains.

I actually cared about my contract, and I didn't want to get into any trouble just because somebody discriminated against me. And I really believe in equality. I don't think anyone has the right to tell someone they can't do something. I will not stand for that bullshit. Somebody has to speak up for the soldiers. That's why I stayed in. I stayed in and became a stronger person thanks to the discrimination and crooked crap I had to deal with.

Sarah began helping out around the unit. When others were taking their breaks, she took on technical tasks around the office: digitizing files, creating rosters, and assisting the unit administrator with the computer functions that confounded him. She demonstrated her mettle in all the physical duties required of her too. After five years, Sarah was promoted to squad leader. The roles were reversed—she was now in command of the same sergeant who had wanted to smoke her until she quit.

Her advancement could not have happened had all of Sarah's superiors been misogynists. Indeed, the U.S. military's trajectory seems inclined toward progress with regard to matters of gender and sexuality. In 2011, President Barack Obama signed into law the repeal of the "Don't Ask, Don't Tell" policy, allowing gays and lesbians to be open and honest in their service. Two years later, the prohibition on women's combat roles was ordered lifted.

But Sarah's encounters with discrimination never ceased either. With good reason, the issue of women in the military is often linked in our minds to rape and sexual assault. Former Secretary of Defense Leon Panetta estimated that about nineteen thousand incidents of sexual assault occurred in the U.S. military in 2011 alone; 95 percent of the victims were women.[21] While unacceptably pervasive, sexual assault is only the most dramatic of the sexist practices occurring in this highly hierarchical and patriarchal institution. Underneath is a wide and deep layer of discrimination experienced every day by soldiers like Sarah, with abuses ranging from the abrasive remarks of superiors and colleagues to systemic staffing discrimination, challenges to promotions, and unjustified assumptions regarding qualifications, among others. When Sarah was up for promotion, for instance, her board included a man accused of raping three women in the army. Although two of the women had dropped their charges, one had not. "So this accused rapist is one of the people who got to decide whether or not I got promoted. It was just nerve-wracking." That scenario is at once quotidian and criminal.

Undeterred, Sarah moved on and up. After eight years in the reserve, she was serving as a full-time staff member in the army and a sergeant in the Active Guard Reserve, thereby becoming even more of a leader to her soldiers. She implemented new policies to improve their experience. For example, whereas soldiers traditionally are counseled when they have done something wrong, Sarah initiated positive monthly counseling sessions, in which she discusses with each soldier his or her performance, development, professional growth, and goals. "I just hope it makes them feel like they're important, because they are. I will do everything for them that I possibly can." Almost a decade ago, the reserve lent Sarah a hand to raise herself out of insecurity. Now she's reaching hers out to others.

. . .

When I spoke with Mike,* he was a relatively new member of the army reserve. His father was in the Special Forces in Vietnam and a combat engineer, but that example was not Mike's motivation. In fact, he saw his father only four times in his life. When Mike was two years old, the family home caught on fire. His parents' marriage was a casualty of the destruction. Thereafter, his father consistently avoided child support payments and alimony to his ex-wife. Mike's grandmother cared for him at home while his mother worked. By the time he was finishing high school, his mother was tiring and Mike had taken over almost all the bills. That made the army recruiter's offer appear especially attractive.

For the first two years, active duty was challenging but exciting. After a year of advanced training, Mike received a secret security clearance and was sent to Korea. "It was amazing. We got to explore all of South Korea; the food was amazing. I made a lot of friends, really good people. I picked up a little language; the Koreans were really nice, and smart with electronics." Mike was advancing in the ranks too, and his first sergeant encouraged the progress. Soon, he was ready to go to the promotional board to become a noncommissioned officer.

"Then the Red Cross message came." Mike's mother was seriously ill. Three days after Mike received this message, his mother passed away from esophageal cancer. Mike never went in front of the promotional board. Instead, he returned home. He began training in one of the United States's domestic army installations. Soon thereafter, his unit was deployed to Iraq.

Trained to conduct detainee operations, Mike's experience in Iraq was "draining and long." He offered me snippets: quelling prison riots with stunner grenades and pepper spray foggers, shooting at an escaping prisoner with riot rounds, working a thirty-eight-hour shift when a prisoner escaped. During that last one, "I was just completely delusional; I didn't even know my own name I was so tired." Long shifts and little time off were the norm. So was "sweating through your boots" in the desert heat. Yet perhaps even more disaffecting than the mission itself was the prevailing "drill sergeant mentality." Mike defines it as "a raw dog mentality that says 'I've got the biggest bark, fuck you!'" He told me regretfully that he acquired that mentality too.

Mike felt damaged enough by five years of active duty, and especially wartime deployment, that he wanted to leave the military for good. When he reached this part of his story, I was prepared for it. Previously, I had spoken with a sergeant who had seen many young soldiers like Mike burn out from deployments to Iraq and Afghanistan. Where Mike was too reticent to wrench my heart with the reasons, Sergeant Smith* filled in the spaces with his own story.

Born and raised in Ohio, Sergeant Smith had been in the U.S. Army for nearly three decades when we spoke. His father was in the military for even longer; and he would be happy to see his teenage daughter continue the tradition, though preferably in the air force. For nearly an hour, he fondly reminisced about his career, demonstrating a sense of pride in a duty fulfilled. Only in the last moments of our conversation did he begin to hint at that which haunts, at that which Mike would not divulge.

Sergeant Smith was deployed to Iraq as a medic soon after the 2003 invasion. There, a man died in his arms. The man was Iraqi, "but they were all just people." Smith's convoy had been stuck in a messy traffic jam in a dangerous neighborhood around Baghdad. The car behind the convoy seemed to be having brake problems, but the tense young officer with Smith lost his judgment and his nerve. "It was a negligent fire incident. It was meant to be a warning shot, but we weren't supposed to fire *any* warning shots." Smith is candid as hell with me: "As far as I'm concerned, we murdered him." The officer's fifty-caliber bullet hit the ground, then, with all its force, ricocheted up through the vehicle into the passenger's groin, and finally out through his arm. Smith and the other medics rushed to treat him. They asked the victim personal questions. Sergeant Smith will never forget the answer to a question about his family: "six daughters, all under fourteen years old." Even while dressing his wounds, Smith knew the man would die: with the force of a fifty-caliber bullet, "everything would be hamburger inside." It was amazing he was even answering those questions.

Smith still sees that man's face every night. He has trouble sleeping and has taken to drink. "Not a day goes by I don't think about what more I could have done . . . maybe if I tried harder." The man's six daughters come to his mind on those sleepless nights: *all under fourteen years old.* Smith has been dealing with his drinking problem himself. He's afraid that if he goes to an army psychologist, he'd be risking his job security. Despite the trauma of his deployment, Smith did not want to lose his job. Nor was he especially sympathetic to young people like Mike, who found in deployment excuses for leaving the army.

In the latter years of the wars in Iraq and Afghanistan, young recruits were increasingly dropping out after deployment. It was "a huge problem for the reserves," according to the sergeant. Smith considers the trend symptomatic "of the society we live in":

> Twenty years ago, when you signed that contract you might as well have signed it in blood. But now, it's almost like it's a living document to some people. They feel that things were different in their life when they signed and it doesn't apply anymore. I think it's a societal and generational thing. It's this generation . . . it's really bad. The younger crowd, once they face some challenges, deploy them or something, then that contract goes out the window. Maybe it's a lack of respect for authority. Or just a lack of honor.

To a young recruit like Mike, dishonor was better than deployment.

Mike was, in any case, content to be "hyping down" from the drill sergeant mentality; almost three years on from active duty, he may finally be "back to normal." Because he had three years left on his contract, Mike intended to ease his way out through the inactive

Individual Ready Reserve, in which he would remain technically a member of the reserve, without pay or training obligations, until or unless activated. In the meantime, he enrolled in welding school and looked for a job. But recruiters kept calling. Mike told them he wanted to move on with his career, but they persisted. So Mike made a deal: he would join the active reserve on condition of no deployment.†

Between school, work, and the reserve, Mike is back to long shifts. Better than war.

· · ·

War brought Marc to America. When he was five years old, Marc's father was making arrangements to extract his family from the madness of Lebanon's civil war, which began in 1975 and lasted fifteen long years. One day in April 1983, he applied at the U.S. Embassy in Beirut for a visa to travel to the United States, where he intended to get a job and make enough money to bring over Marc and the family. The visa was stamped. An hour after Marc's father left the building, a militant protesting the intervention of U.S. forces in Lebanon drove his van into the embassy, blowing up himself and more than sixty other people.

Over the next year, as Lebanese, Israeli, Palestinian, Syrian, American, and French warriors tore Marc's country to pieces, his father washed dishes furiously at Little Caesars Pizza in northeastern Ohio. He got his foot in the door of the chain's local branch, thanks to an older brother in the restaurant business in Cleveland. On the other side of the ocean, Marc's family secured temporary protective status to enter the United States, thanks largely to their Christian heritage. Eventually, the United States—regretting its entanglement in a for-

---

†I am told that the army reserve is not in a position to make such a guarantee to its recruits. It could be that Mike misunderstood the conditions of his contract, or that the army, or at least a particular recruiter, had his or her own reasons for conceding to Mike's condition.

eign war—withdrew its forces from Lebanon. Soon after, Marc and his mother—fearing daily for their lives—pulled up their roots and came to the United States.

Another Lebanese family had long since settled in the area. Years before Marc's family relocated, Diana's father had immigrated to America as one of the more traditional deprived masses called upon by Lady Liberty: he sought economic opportunity. With little education and even less money, he found support from other Lebanese living on Cleveland's west side. Together they operated a gas station. He never saw most of each dollar he made, promptly sending his earnings to his siblings and parents back home. When he had just enough savings, he flew back to his village in Lebanon, met and married a recently widowed young woman, and brought her back to Ohio to start a family. Together they would have two boys and two girls, including Diana. In this new chapter in his life, Diana's father landed a position as a transmissions specialist at General Motors. With the post came a living wage, benefits, and security; "the union was obviously a huge part of that," Diana notes. He worked second shift for decades, leaving to work when the kids were just coming home from school, coming home when they were sound asleep.

When Diana and Marc met as young adults, their worlds melded easily. When they speak of their parents' journeys from Lebanon, and their own childhoods in the United States, their harmony is manifest.

MARC: My dad had like eighty bucks in his pocket when he came.

DIANA: My dad nearly starved to death, he wasn't making much and supporting his siblings and parents back home.

MARC: It's focus on Parent, Protector, and Provider.

DIANA: Dad always told us, "I work hard for you to have a better life."

MARC: The obvious stereotypes were a lot harsher back then. People didn't know, and they were scared of what they didn't know.

DIANA: Americans were scared because they knew [immigrants] were going to work ten times harder to get what they need.

MARC: My parents pounded in Lebanese culture.

DIANA: Family. That's why I say we lived in a bubble—it was all family.

MARC: I had a great childhood because of my dad. I remember him telling me, "This is what I worked hard for."

DIANA: My dad is very proud of what he's accomplished. He always says, "I never had the education. You have that opportunity."

MARC: I can't imagine what my parents went through, coming here at that age.

DIANA: I look at myself compared to them, and I feel so lazy, thinking about what they went through. It makes me sick.

The dreams of the parents were planted in the children. When Marc and Diana awoke as adults, they set out to realize those dreams. For Marc, that meant working full-time while pursuing his bachelor's degree. Upon graduation, he explored a number of jobs. But it was "natural" to be drawn back into the restaurant business like the rest of the family. "I did it, was good at it, was lucky to have people in my life that helped me." Along with the inclination, he had acquired the work ethic: "I do everything with passion, whether I'm cooking eggs or running the restaurant. I'm my worst self-critic. I think that's all tied into our culture—that sense of paranoia." Now he's a managing partner at a local Italian restaurant that has grown from two to six units in the three years he has been there.

But America wavered in her offerings of opportunity along the way. Working for a catering company prior to joining the restaurant, Marc and his team were sensing the effects of the Great Recession and trying to protect the operation from the worst of them: they renegotiated leases, absorbed income losses, and reconceived business models. Meanwhile, staff members were getting depressed as personal earnings shrank, and a habit of drunkenness took hold among many. Then in 2009, Marc and thirty-eight others lost their jobs.

Marc went home to Diana, his wife of not quite three months. Seeing her that day, he asked himself, "What would my dad have done? Would he have sat home and collected unemployment?" Marc got on the phone and solicited everyone he knew. He reached out to his contacts in the Lebanese community, because "people of the same background as you, same standards and work ethic, they vouch for you." In just four days, Marc landed a job as a chef at a steak house. A year later, he secured a position as managing partner at the Italian restaurant where he was working when we met. There he constantly endeavors to maintain a sustainable model in a market unsympathetic to small businesses. Competing against corporate chains that can afford television commercials and ever-longer happy hours, Marc places his faith in "old-school word of mouth, an excellent product, and taking care of the staff so they will take care of your customers." When he tells me his income, I suspect his approach is working.

Diana's dreams were modest and maternal. After high school, she worked a few jobs and received an associate's degree from Cuyahoga Community College. Only when she married Marc, who was always consumed by work, did she take a job as a bank teller for "something to do." After they had their first child—a girl they successfully convince me is brilliant beyond her age—Diana chose to stay home from work. She likes staying at home with her daughter—a choice both conservative and fortunate. "We grew up with our mothers home, and I wanted that for her," Diana explains. Marc is more than amenable; the setup fits perfectly his objective of being "parent, protector, provider." With a good deal of pride, he assures me that "everything we do is for her. We don't do anything for ourselves. Everything we do is with our family in mind." The girl seems lucky. Marc wants countless siblings for her, "maybe fifteen" he exclaims, only half jokingly. Diana blushes. "Maybe we'll have one more," she says.

There was no shortage of hardship in Diana's and Marc's backgrounds; their present comfort was generations in the making. But in them I found something rare in my journey around the state: belief in the American Dream. Marc's faith is especially fervent. When he came to America as a young boy, he found a country that was "vast, huge, and beautiful." More than twenty years later, he has concluded that the United States "is definitely the land of opportunity." If people choose not to seize the opportunities on offer, they have themselves to blame. In Lebanon, he notes, those opportunities do not exist in the first place.

A successful immigrant narrative helps justify his optimism in the American Dream. Another standard precept of that dream is the belief that the next generation will be better off. But when a survey asked Americans whether their children will have a better standard of living than themselves, only 38 percent of whites said they believe that will be the case. On the other hand, 64 percent of Hispanics—not Lebanese but an immigrant community with enough numbers to demonstrate the trend—believe their children will be better off. Their optimism extends backward, too. More than 71 percent of Hispanics feel they are better off than their parents (many of whom were immigrants); just over half of whites feel the same way. It happens that blacks are the most optimistic of all. Nearly seven in ten blacks believe their children will enjoy a better standard of living than their own.[22]

Marc's age also inspires his faith in the American Dream. A majority of young Americans believe that their children will be better off than themselves. Less than half of middle-aged folks, and even fewer seniors, believe the same. It may well be the case that this sense of faith in the future dissipates with age. But even if that faith comes with an expiration date, its existence may matter most among the people who are laying their foundations now.

· · ·

Optimism remains a hard sell for many. College costs and student debts are higher than ever, while the economy seems unforgiving even to those with degrees. A more impressive past makes the present (and future) even more discomfiting. Once upon a time, the United States was the world leader in educating its youth. Economists Claudia Goldin and Lawrence Katz have documented the rise and fall of the American educational system. For most of the nineteenth and twentieth centuries, the American system was the most advanced *and* egalitarian system in the world. More Americans at all ages were more educated than people anywhere else in the world, including other rich industrialized nations. Our superior economic performance was testament to the strength of the system.[23]

Beginning in the 1970s, however, our leadership in education began to falter. Rates of high school graduation plateaued; rates of college graduation actually declined for a time, and educational attainment from one generation to the next was increasing at a slower pace than it had for the better part of a century.[24] We did not hit a ceiling: the simultaneous increases in educational attainment and performance in other rich countries demonstrated that our achievement could be surpassed.[25] Our schools now continuously fall behind in the rankings.

In America today, college is bookended by a deteriorating K–12 educational system on one side and debt on the other. Our colleges and universities remain among the best in the world, but not enough people are getting there. Many wonder if the degree is even worth pursuing anymore.

Goldin and Katz insist it is well worth pursuing. A commonly cited explanation for increasing income inequality is that skill-favoring technological change in the modern economy benefits the most highly educated among us (as in, "it's the computers"). Goldin and Katz add an important layer of nuance to this argument. They point out that there is nothing new about technological change or its demand for new skills—the twentieth century was full of technological and industrial advancement. The market has consistently demanded an educated supply of workers. For most of the twentieth century, that supply of workers was expanding and their years of education were increasing. The difference, since the 1980s, is not in the pace of technological change. Rather, the supply of educated workers is not keeping up with the demand for them. Although college enrollment has continued to increase, it has done so too slowly. Education in America has been losing the race against technology. Because those who do get properly educated are in limited supply, the market favors them. We end up then, with income inequality.

Renowned economist Thomas Piketty warns against attributing rising income inequality to the theory proposed by Goldin and Katz, however. He notes that the top 1 percent and .01 percent of Americans accruing massive incomes do not neatly overlap with the top 1 percent and .01 percent of the skilled and educated. Many more Americans than that have a higher education. Moreover, the incomes earned by the top 1 percent are far too high to match any gains in productivity that may result from their level of education.[26] Better, Piketty proposes, to focus on the transformation in societal norms—norms that increasingly favor massive pay packages for top executives and managers.

Even so, a college education certainly improves the lot of those that have one, despite the costs and debt associated with its attainment. The *college wage premium*—that is, the extra wages earned by degree holders compared to those not holding degrees—remains large enough to make higher education pay off. The numbers speak powerfully: since the 1970s, those with a bachelor's degree have earned, on average, 56 percent more than high school graduates; over their lifetimes, those with the degree will earn more than one million dollars more than those without.[27] No matter what one's major or area of study, the payoff persists. Those with associate's degrees likewise receive a higher wage premium than high school graduates, and their investment is worthwhile as well. And even when wages fall, as they did before and after the recession, they fall for everyone—so those with college degrees are still better off. Moreover, the value of higher education also transcends raw economic gains: a more educated citizenry is a more active one; a more educated human being is a more enlightened one.

Thoughtful policies can allow more Americans to benefit from these potential gains. Goldin and Katz propose three places to start: greater access to preschool, improved K–12 schooling, and more generous and transparent financial aid for college.[28] Of course, here we are just touching the surface of the policy debates. Suffice it to say that improving access to and affordability of education for our youth can improve individual lives immensely, and perhaps reduce income inequality. Making America a world leader once again might be an added bonus.

CHAPTER SIX

Not a Desk Job

Fools stand on their island opportunities and look
toward another land. There is no other land; there is
no other life but this, or the like of this.
   —Henry David Thoreau

I'm from Bellevue. It's partially in Huron and then three other counties: Erie, Sandusky, and Seneca. I was born in Sandusky. We originally started going to Iowa in the summer of 2008, stay for three months, then come back and go to college. Then after graduation in 2010, we moved permanently. We graduated from Ohio State University. "We" is my husband.

In Iowa we work for John Deere. There are dealerships in Ohio, but we work at a factory. It's a lot bigger market out there. I'm in customer support and he's an engine engineer. I studied agricultural education at Ohio State. After graduation we were both looking for jobs and the best job offer we got came from Iowa—the most pay. So we actually moved out there. Even though we get paid better, we still have to pay more to live there. Combined we are making a hundred thousand [dollars per year].

My stepdad farms. My dad farms also. My mom is a teacher's aide, works at the school. Actually the one thing that has helped a lot is farming, because the farming markets in the economy have been pretty strong the last couple years. So even though the economy is hurting, the agriculture industry is pretty strong. That's helped. I think that with the drought coming this year it will drive the prices up, so it'll help: we'll

*get higher prices for crops that we do have. And then we'll just have to
take crop insurance for the yields that we don't get this year.*

*I would say we were middle class. Actually, going through college,
I got most of it paid through financial aid. We didn't really have a lot,
and what we had we always re-invested on the farm.*

*I thought about working on the farm. My stepdad told me I could
be the farm manager if I wanted to. I'm not really . . . working with
family is not something I want to do. I don't want to drive, you know,
drive nails in between when we don't need to. Sometimes working with
family causes more problems than it's worth. I did think about staying
in the area to teach because my degree is in education. But my husband
is an engineer, obviously would get paid a lot more than I do, so we let
him find a job first and then I decided I could teach wherever or get a
job somewhere else in the ag-related industry.*

—Megan, 25, Huron County

With smooth fair skin filled by a plump frame, Megan looks younger
than her years. Her cheeks redden faintly under her freckles when she
shares her news: she's pregnant. She is happy about this, and I find
myself excited for her. I also add it to the list of Megan's attainments:
a college degree, a husband, a job, and a house. As she matured into
the adult that sat before me, Megan had done something common
among the children of farmers—she declined to become one.

Though he does not know Megan, James* would be familiar with,
and sympathetic to, her choice. After all, none of his five children
are in farming. He appreciates that his grown children "know all the
hard times I had: two-dollar corn, three-dollar corn, trying to pay
for the farm and raise five kids. Sometimes you just didn't make it.
They said they want no part of it." To make it, James's wife, Linda,*
has worked an administrative job in a trucking company for most
of the last thirty years. That's not all. James has a small machine
shop "on the side," and Linda works as a school officer too. Their
careers are etched onto their faces: Linda's pillowy white skin reflects
the static fluorescent-lit walls of an office, while James's dark and

deeply lined countenance betrays years in the sun and the fields. The children—with fourteen kids of their own—resemble their mother. James's children stayed in Ohio; Megan left. All contributed to the same trends: American farmers are growing fewer and older. In 1997, the average farmer was fifty-four years old; in 2007, he was fifty-seven. Three out of five American farm operators are over fifty-five years of age; one in four is over sixty-five, a group that has been expanding since the 1960s.[1] In Ohio, that demographic is even bigger: one in three farm operators is over sixty-five.[2] It is worth remembering that we are only talking about the 1 percent of the American population that claims farming as an occupation at all.[3]

And that number is dwindling too. The number of farms in America reached its peak a long time ago, in 1935; at that time, America had nearly seven million farms. In 2012, slightly more than two million remained. In Ohio, the number of farms nearly halved from 135,000 farms in 1963 to 73,400 farms by 2012. Some may rush to attribute the decline in the real number of farms to the rise of "mega" or corporate farms. But the average U.S. farm size has increased by only about one hundred acres in the last forty years, to an average of 421 acres in 2012. In Ohio, the average farm size is just 185 acres. Indeed, only 4 percent of all U.S. farms are "corporate" farms, although many large "family farms" operate on the same scale and are, de facto, corporate too. Other developments in the industry, such as large-scale mechanization and the commercialization of fertilizer and pesticides, have diminished the need for more farmers.[4] Counting the costs of doing business is one useful way to comprehend the decline of the American farmer.

Let's keep this brief. The U.S. Census Bureau deems an establishment a farm if it produces and sells one thousand dollars or more of agricultural products in a year. Meanwhile, farm production expenses average more than one *hundred* thousand dollars per year. Most farmers are not breaking even—the median household income from farming was negative from 2009 to 2013. Most of the average total income of farm households, $68,298, is actually made by other means.[5] The farmers of big farms are naturally better positioned to meet their expenses and make a profit, while those running small farms earn their money elsewhere. That's why a minority of farms accounts for the majority of sales.[6] And for those wondering, the answer is yes—government subsidies are included in sales. We will revisit that issue later.

These statistics explain why farming is not the principal occupation of most farmers. With about one and a half jobs each, James and Linda embody this reality. Not even half of farmers identify farming as their principal occupation.

Let's meet two farmers whose sole occupation *is* farming. First there is Dave, whose corn and soybeans—low on nutrients and cost alike—have him faring pretty well as a medium-sized farmer. And then there is Daniel, who participates in a local food movement by selling organic berries and honey; without his wife's income, Daniel's farming probably would not be sustainable.

· · ·

Dave reduces everything I laid out above to three words: "Farming is hard." In his early fifties, Dave works seven days a week on five thousand acres in Ross County, Ohio. But for a few overnight stays in different parts of the state, he has not taken a vacation since 1992. That was the year Dave learned a lesson. After driving through the night down to Myrtle Beach, South Carolina, he and his wife checked into their hotel room and found the phone light blinking. He called back home to learn that six inches of rain had caused his water gaps to go out. "I was about to have livestock scattered everywhere!" So Dave and his wife got right back into their car and drove north to Ohio in the middle of the night. He told her he would never leave again. "And I haven't," he confirms. He admits that as somebody with almost no time off work, he is "probably a candidate for a short life."

I am grateful Dave has made time in his schedule for our conversation. Actually, as I sit across the table from him, with a bowl of pistachios between us that he never touches and I never neglect, I realize Dave is happy to be talking with me. I need not speculate much about why—he loves what he does and is pleased to translate his passion into lessons and stories for someone who will listen. An added bonus to an already easy session is how much Dave looks the part: in his jeans and plaid flannel shirt, his cap on his knee (it came off the gentleman's head the moment he walked through the door), Dave seems to me the quintessence of an American farmer. With aviator glasses (old-fashioned face-dominating prescription eyewear, not intentionally trendy), thinning hair, and a paunch cultivated over decades, he also embodies the aging farmer demographic. At least in his maturity he has accepted the need for health insurance.

Dave pays for farming with more than his health. The costs of his operations have been increasing steadily for years. "I'm a small farmer," he begins.

There's a lot of big operations and bigger operations—mega-farms, twenty to thirty thousand acres. The bigger farmers can buy inputs cheaper: they buy more of it in volume. The reason the smaller farmers are leaving is the economics: you cannot make a profit enough to survive. You either have a supplemental income or a wife that had a good job. Those are getting fewer and fewer because it's hard work, it's long hours, and the prices. Everything is volume. This year, [a corporation] bid on a farm against me. The landlord was good enough to come and tell me, and we worked out an arrangement. She didn't want them.

Dave is keeping up pretty well, aided by his two part-time employees and some very good machinery ("It's cheaper to rely on a piece of equipment than it is an employee; the machine doesn't call in sick, doesn't have a ball game to go to . . ."). These days, before paying taxes, Dave makes more than $150,000 per year. His income wasn't always that high, but it was generally quite good. Despite high costs, hard work can still produce a fair reward, it seems. For the younger generation, however, the input is not worth the outcome. Dave renders my research unnecessary, readily reciting the data on the age of the average farmer in America. And he provides the analysis, too—the economic challenges, and the generational question. His short answer to the latter: "Kids today have very little ambition."

Back when Dave was young, he and the other boys in the area used to knock on the neighbors' doors and offer to bale hay. Today, if you ask the boys to bale hay (for money, mind you), "they'll laugh at you," Dave says. They will play football all summer, "bust their ass for no money," but refuse work. Of course there are exceptions, but even the willing workers do not have the stamina: "couple of hours, they're burnt out." Training and education are largely to blame. The schools are not teaching them skills for the workforce except "how to use computers and how to work sitting on your ass." Woodshops and other vocational training programs are increasingly scarce, and the kids are uninterested anyway: "Everyone wants a college education and a desk job." Dave believes that this problem extends to other industries too. Students in college are not taught to operate the advanced machinery used in today's factories, for example.

"So what's going to happen?" Dave asks. "Jobs are going to go overseas." His neighbors complain that they don't want immigrants in Ohio, but the difference between immigrants and Americans is that "Mexicans will work."

All of this is especially disturbing to Dave because it contrasts sharply with the path he walked in life. In 1968, Dave's mother and little brother died in a car accident, leaving Dave's father with six children. The youngest was seven-year-old Dave. The family lived on a small farm, although Dave's father did not make his primary living from it—the land was for raising the children, along with fifty cows and a hundred acres of crops. Dave took to the farm, and it took to Dave. He used to feed the cows in the morning, walk to school, and return to do chores on the farm through the afternoon and evening. At ten years old, he knew that he wanted to spend his life on the land. At fifteen, he had to. His father grew too ill to do much of anything, and by then the other children were grown and starting their own families; not one of them went into agriculture. So Dave "took over everything." With two years of high school left, he enrolled in vocational training for agricultural mechanics. His father hoped he would go to college, but Dave was "too bull-headed; I knew what I wanted to do, and I just went out and did it." By the time I met him, Dave was running sixteen farms, spanning five thousand acres.

Of the sixteen farms, Dave owns four. He manages seven others on a "cash-rent basis," meaning he pays rent to the landowners, covers the expenses, and all crop output and income is his. The remaining five farms are run on a "fifty-fifty sharecropping basis." This is the "fairest" setup: the landlord furnishes the land, while Dave pays half the inputs and furnishes the machinery, the fuel, and the labor; when the crop is sold the income is split in equal parts between them. These arrangements make Dave a "non-family farmer," according to the American Farm Bureau Federation. Of eight farm types, this one constitutes just 4 percent of farms but produces more than 20 percent of total farm sales. In other words, it is a fairly lucrative arrangement. For Dave, it was his only way to farm on a profitable scale.

Large tracts of land are inherited (or else bought at prohibitive prices), and, these days, much of that land passes through families that do not want to farm themselves. Many large landowners "are away from agriculture, don't even live near the farm. They are more comfortable with just 'show me the money.' That is the wave now," Dave explains. It is one of the reasons younger people who are not born into farming do not enter it.

My meeting with Dave took place on one of the farms he manages on a sharecropping basis. This farm does not have a high crop yield— oaks, maples, and other hardwoods cover most of the acreage—but Dave raises sixty of his beef cows on the landlord's pastureland. I was excited to learn a few things about the livestock (did you know cows are pregnant for nine months, like humans, and that hogs are pregnant for three months, three weeks, and three days?) and to be spending a few nights in these bucolic environs.

The owner of the land was not a farmer himself, just a man drawn to nature. In the 1960s, he moved with his wife and children into the grand mid-nineteenth-century barn, built of the same trees that carpet most of their five hundred acres. After seeing four children and eleven grandchildren into the world, he passed away. His wife remains alone in their home, carving slabs of wood into pieces of art, giving generously of her time to social causes, and looking forward to the next visit from her grandchildren. Since none of her children went into farming, there was nothing for them in that town. My own visit was facilitated through her brother, an older colleague. When I pulled into her dirt road from the main street, I was enveloped by rolling hills, greeted by horses and dogs, and warmed by the wood of late November. I hugged this woman, still a stranger to me, and noted that during my three-day stay I would be living better than almost everyone in that town—except the other landowners.

Spread over Dave's other farms are three thousand acres of crops, half corn and half soybeans on a fifty-fifty rotation, as "you have less disease problems that way." In 2011, the value of production for these two crops in Ohio was $6.8 billion. In contrast, fruit and vegetable production in the state was valued at $155 million.[7] The market's distaste for greens conjures for me an image of a three-year-old refusing to eat his veggies. But behind every high-fructose-corn-syrup-loving child is the hand (not so "invisible," we'll see) that feeds it.

Most of Dave's soybeans are sold overseas, especially to Asia. As their country's economy has grown and developed, the Chinese "found out they needed protein, because their people wanted to eat better." Soybean meal is fed to hogs and other livestock, animals that Chinese people really like to eat now that they can afford to. Back in the 1980s and early 1990s, Dave tells me, "Soybeans were selling at five to seven dollars [per bushel]. Now we are in the eleven– to fifteen-dollar range."

Fortunately for him, the price of corn has also increased significantly. Most of Dave's corn is sold to livestock farmers for feed. Still, Dave recognizes the role of ethanol in raising the value of this crop. "Before ethanol, we were selling corn for three dollars a bushel. Almost overnight, it went to five dollars. About four years ago, midway into Bush, he announced that act—it was a big boost for us economically." Dave is referring to the 2007 Energy Independence and Security Act, which mandates the blending of corn-based ethanol into gasoline, aiming to reduce the nation's dependence on foreign oil and lessen carbon emissions. Aside from dramatically increasing the price of corn and enhancing the livelihoods of farmers and agribusinesses that hardly needed the boost, the desired effects of corn ethanol have yet to manifest themselves. Moreover, the production of corn ethanol consumes valuable water resources; in coming years, climate change is expected to hasten the need for more water for the production of corn ethanol, even while reducing corn yields.[8] More immediately, diverting corn crops to biodiesel reduces our exports to the world food market,[9] an effect that drove up prices during the global food crisis in 2008, and again in 2012, when a drought struck America's Midwest. It was during the latter that I spoke with Dave; he was making seven to eight dollars per bushel of corn.

Dave wants us to be clear about a few things, however. First, he believes that corn would hold its own without the government mandate. Second, while prices are up, so are costs. "Our prices have quadrupled on the income side, but they have also quadrupled on the expense side. We are really no better off now than we were when corn was two dollars a bushel. We are sort of in the same plateau, just handling more dollars." For anyone to think otherwise is just one example of "miscommunication between the public and farmers," Dave insists. Another misunderstanding, he adds, is the notion that government subsidies unjustly favor and protect American farmers.

"Let's break this down," Dave begins. He addresses first the government subsidies provided to farmers, deemed by critics America's "largest corporate welfare program." The commodity provisions in the

U.S. farm bill support farmers by paying them for crops regardless of the amount and rate of production. The intent is to support farmers even when the free market and nature do not. Because payments are capped, Dave insists it is not as problematic as the critics contend.

However, most of the money, even if capped, is going to the farmers who need it the least. In 2007, a third of government payments went to Ohio farms with revenues exceeding $500,000.[10] The distortion also extends to the type of crops grown, with 90 percent of payments subsidizing just five crops: wheat, cotton, corn, soybeans, and rice—all corporate farm favorites.[11] The commodity programs also allow farmers to borrow money from the government at very low interest rates. Dave explains that people rightly get "pissed off" because the money borrowed often *appears* to be part of farmers' incomes. "Another misconception," he laments.

And while these farmer support programs are big—amounting to nearly $87 billion from 2008 to 2012—they are only part of the story. "What people don't know is that food stamps and school lunches come out of that farm bill." Dave is right. From 2008 to 2012, spending on the Supplemental Nutrition Assistance Program (SNAP, formerly known as food stamps) was around $314 billion.[12] The farm bill is a poorly named behemoth, encompassing so many programs (granted, mostly related to things we put in our mouths) that lawmakers can hardly deal with it. The divisions on Capitol Hill do not fall neatly along partisan lines: social progressives and fiscal conservatives both want to eliminate or reduce subsidies to farmers (with the latter wanting to do the same to food stamp provisions).

When the 2008 farm bill expired in 2012, Congress was too divided to enact a new bill; the old one was renewed for another year. The politicians remained deadlocked over the issue through 2013, but in 2014, they finally agreed to a ten-year, $956 billion bill. Everyone took a cut after the divisive debates: the new farm bill will spend $8 billion less on food stamp and nutrition programs and $14 billion less on farmer commodities (subsidies). Crop insurance was increased as a concession to the farmers.[13]

Amid the wrangling in Washington, farm lobbyists and rural politicians favoring subsidies amplify voices like Dave's. Indeed, they feel unduly victimized in the debates, given the provisions benefiting the food stamp program. Dave vents, though in an unperturbed manner:

> The bad thing is on the farm bill, there's a thing called pork. That's how come the food stamps and school lunch program is in the agriculture bill—that's how they get it to pass. If you're trying to pass a farm bill, for farming only, there's not enough people in Washington who give a shit to vote for it. So that's why they have to put in the other stuff. The actual public have no way of figuring that stuff out. There's no one out there to educate them. Farm Bureau is doing some, but they can't knock on every door. They just need to get the people in Washington educated.

The Farm Bureau is the American Farm Bureau Federation, the largest farmers' interest group in the country. The lobbying group refers to itself as the "voice of agriculture."

Dave may think that the position of the farm lobby is not widely understood, but it does seem to be heard well enough by many legislators, who continue to promote farm subsidies while attacking the food stamp program. Indeed, while the farm bill remained divisive, lawmakers agreed for long enough to allow for the expiration of SNAP benefits that had been increased under the 2009 Recovery Act. Despite cutbacks to the program, nearly 15 percent of Ohio's population, one in seven Ohioans, relied on food stamps in 2014.[14]

The lobby aside, Dave is speaking in his own voice, one that is informed and invested. As a former president of both the local Cattlemen's Association and the local Farmer's Club, Dave grapples with these issues even when he's not in the fields.

· · ·

Daniel's experience with farming is like Dave's: taxing. "I'm often sore, wet, cold, and miserable." Also like Dave, Daniel finds the physical toll compounded by the financial investment: "Farming is tough and making a living at farming is tough. It's a lot of risk; there are so many variables you can't control. A lot of farmers, either they themselves work off the farm or their spouse works off the farm— that makes it possible." The latter applies to Daniel. His wife works for the Ohio branch of a multinational corporation. That makes for an apparent incongruence in their respective professional interests, but in fact there is an important interdependence between them. Daniel thinks he could still run the farm without his wife's income, "but it would be a lot scarier, a lot more difficult." It helps, too, that he and his wife decided not to have children.

For Daniel, farming is harder still because of the very policies that favor Dave. As discussed above, federal farm subsidies are skewed toward supporting large-scale farming and a few select crops, mostly grains ("the worst foods for you," Daniel laments). Since Daniel is producing organic fruits and vegetables, the policy bias in favor of big grain injures not only his pockets but his principles. He believes strongly in personal involvement, on both individual and community levels, in producing the food we eat. That is what got him into this whole business in the first place.

Daniel's farm is in Peninsula, in a region between Cleveland and Akron that is home to the Cuyahoga Valley National Park. The park contains woods, farmland, waterfalls, the Ohio & Erie Canal, and the legendary Cuyahoga River. The region is a "jewel that so many people don't even know about," Daniel notes. That is probably true; perhaps I was fortunate that my father used to take my siblings and me on day trips to the park. We would bike along the Towpath Trail that follows the route of the 1820s hand-dug canal; the canal locks along the way were special treats for exploration. It was a pleasure to encounter the region anew, especially the farmland, when I visited Daniel. It was a warm autumn day and he brought out two chairs and set them outside the old barn, allowing us unhindered indulgence in nature's production. Rows of raspberries, cabbages, and pumpkins stretched before us, with a curtain of trees displaying the oranges and yellows of the season in the background and a 1940s tractor in the foreground, stage right. "On a day like today," Daniel says, "it's great to be a farmer."

Juxtapose this environment with the one where Daniel grew up, in Youngstown, Ohio. In the early twentieth century, the Youngstown area boasted the "largest concentration of steel-making facilities per capita, and per square mile, in the world," and was the nation's largest steel producer after Pittsburgh.[15] The Mahoning River, connecting this corner of Ohio to the wider world, served as the passageway for industrialization. When Daniel was a child, the steel was already turning to rust, although Daniel was too young to comprehend the deepening deindustrialization around him. "Kids don't think in terms of employment and people working in the mills," he reflects these many years later. "I was always like a little environmentalist. I saw the smokestacks and thought, 'That's not a good thing.'" By the time Daniel was in college, discussions of Youngstown's steelmaking were conducted in the past tense.

Daniel's father did not work in steel. He owned a furniture store and later managed a fireworks plant. However, his businesses, like those of many people in town, depended on the economic vibrancy and middle-class incomes provided by the mills. While Daniel's father worked, his mother stayed at home and raised their three children, who "did pretty good on birthdays and never felt deprived of anything." Their neighborhood was composed primarily of blue-collar workers of European descent, mostly Italians. Youngstown was once a prime destination for immigrants, who were drawn to the jobs in the steel industry. In the thirty years between 1890 and 1920 alone, the city's population grew by about one hundred thousand people; more than one out of every four of them was foreign-born.[16] Though diversity was substantial, ethnic mixing was limited. Many of the area's neighborhoods were ethnic and racial enclaves, a characteristic compounded by corporate management policies that provided company housing in a manner that solidified class and ethnic divisions.[17] By the time Daniel was in high school, the groups composing Youngstown's population had melded to some degree, but not enough for blacks to enter the mix. Buses had to bring them in.

In the late 1980s, Daniel began studying philosophy at Youngstown State University. He paid for his education with money he made selling fireworks for his dad. He came out with no debt and a new girlfriend, who would become his wife. Although he never felt particularly fortunate back then, Daniel looks back gratefully. "I was able to work and go to school and it was affordable. It's something I'm very concerned about, people strapped with debt for decades after getting out of college. Makes you wonder whether it's worth it or not. I mean, education is always a good thing. And it makes for better citizens. But it's hard to justify being strapped like that." Education wasn't just a good thing for Daniel—it was his primary thing. He went on to receive a master's degree in education at Kent State University and then taught elementary school for a few years. "I went to all public schools and state universities; I owe a debt of gratitude to the public school systems, and I don't forget it," he points out. But from the classroom his eyes were always straining to look outside the window. Eventually, they pulled him into a Ph.D. program at Kent State University, where he wrote a dissertation on the philosophy of environmental education, drawing on the written works of Henry David Thoreau, Aldo Leopold, and E. O. Wilson.

After a few years of teaching at the university level, the outdoors began to tug at Daniel again. He asked himself what he wanted to do with his life, and how he could do it outdoors, on the land. Thoreau answered him. For it was Thoreau whose "philosophy, his idea, was that he was going to live with a piece of land and live his life for all that it was worth. That it was going to be real. If it was hard it was going to be hard, but he was going to live it and experience it."

So Daniel followed Thoreau into the woods. As he was completing his doctoral dissertation, he submitted a proposal to a new program of the Cuyahoga Valley National Park offering old farms on parkland for lease to individuals interested in small-scale, sustainable farming. The location would allow Daniel to enjoy city life when he wanted and remain near relatives in Youngstown. He secured a sixty-year lease on twenty acres of land and began a Community Supported Agriculture (CSA) program.

CSAs, which have proliferated in recent years alongside urban farming and farmers markets, allow members of a community to "buy in" to a local farmer's production costs and receive part of the harvest in return. By paying up front, community members assume some of the risk of a bad harvest but also reap the benefits of locally grown organic food and the enjoyment of being involved in its production. The nearly one hundred families who pick up their weekly basket of food from Daniel get to be "in touch with the food and to taste what food tastes like when it's freshly picked, know what goes into it, including the trials and tribulations of farming, of which there are quite a bit." And Daniel makes sure his members' baskets don't go empty. He works with other local farmers if he has a bad week, and they do likewise.

The CSA crops range from bok choy to cherry tomatoes, but Daniel's two loves are his berries and his bees. "We just extracted honey last week," he happily reports. He regularly opens the farm to the community for berry picking, "another way for people to come and experience and appreciate the land." When I visited him the following spring, during one of the season's events, children picked berries in the field while folk musicians picked at banjoes and fiddles. Neighbors grilled squash and squeezed lemons into lemonade. It was more than delightful—it was Daniel's dream.

In principle, Daniel is deriving satisfaction from the endeavor. After spending years unfulfilled in the classroom, he is more content to be engaged in physical production. "In an ideal world, I would like to see more craftsmen, artisans, and farmers, working and making a good living at that type of work—*real* work," he explains. He contrasts this with the type of jobs held by financiers and bankers, or by corporate managers who compensate their employees poorly while making historically high salaries themselves. Daniel's earnings come from hard work and saving. He is proud of that.

Like a dream, though, the enjoyment can be fleeting. The work embodies his ideals but it is hardly idyllic. Sometimes Daniel must remind himself that Thoreau never said it would be easy. And then there is the incessant discontent that is the fate of the politicized, as Daniel surely is. As with his work, Daniel takes an active approach to his politics. He gets involved with electoral campaigns and Democratic politics, "driven by the [idea] that we are all in it together." Yet unrequited ideals beget frustration. The riches of the rich and the power of the powerful have been increasing ceaselessly over the course of Daniel's adulthood. And now that he has inserted himself into a tireless and financially thankless profession, watching all the while the rise in income enjoyed by corporate farmers, the disappointment is worse still.

Daniel points his finger toward a corner of his farm and shares with me his idea of building a small cabin there. In it, he wants to write a book, to put into words these ruminations. From the books to the land, and back again.

· · ·

In his corner of Appalachia in eastern Ohio, Greg also contemplates the land. On the surface, he sees his chestnut trees, and beyond them the other crops and woods overlying the rolling hills of Carroll County. That which lies beneath the land—shale—is in his mind's eye, too.

"When I look at a piece of land, I kind of turn the clock back and then turn it forward," Greg says. The journey in time begins with his father, who had a "tree hobby." While raising Greg and his siblings in Canton, he bought a piece of land about forty miles southeast of the city, in Carroll County, bordering West Virginia and Pennsylvania. Lamenting that "'farmers cut down trees to farm,' he vowed to do otherwise." Starting in 1958, he planted several varieties of trees. The chestnuts, especially, thrived. By the early 1970s, trees had become Greg's hobby. He and his father focused on cultivating the chestnuts, which soon spread over all their acreage. Greg pursued his education, even receiving his Ph.D. in forestry. Still, chestnuts were his future. "My dad's hobby got out of control, and now it's my business," he quips.

Business is good for Greg. Chestnuts are scarcely grown in the United States—his is one of the few commercial-sized chestnut orchards in the country—and demand is high. Greg hardly needs to promote his business—he's busy just trying to fill orders. Most of those orders come from immigrant communities in the United States accustomed to chestnuts in their diet, including Koreans, Chinese, Serbians, and Bosnians. "Probably 75 percent end up in the home of a Korean," Greg estimates. His customers prefer his fresh crop to the imported varieties that lose quality by the time they arrive in the United States. After Greg drove me up and down the hills of the orchard in his white Ford pickup, he treated me to some chestnuts. My family always roasts them in wintertime, but this was my first taste of the raw nut. The body and the flavor were hardy; like its purveyor, it had an overtone of sweetness. "I don't make much money, but I do get letters of appreciation. That's worth something." I also wrote Greg a thank-you letter.

As business grew, Greg sought a sustainable way to expand. In 2009, his chestnut trees produced sixty thousand pounds of nuts: "too much." As usual, he hired pickers from the area to gather the crop, about a third of them Amish. "I'd rather be paying in to people's hands than paying for a machine to pick the chestnuts," Greg opines. Despite the people to pick, the 2009 harvest was too large to process. Thus by the next year, Greg had built a new processing facility. He also persuaded three other landowners to enter into a co-op, a cooperative agreement. The other co-op members would hire the hands to pick the crop, which Greg would then purchase and process. Before this venture, the other landowners hadn't invested in farming the land; they had bought it to hunt. But with Greg as their neighbor, they became chestnut growers too.

Before Greg started the co-op, an unexpected party tried to become his partner in the chestnut business: a coal mining company. A strip of grassland runs along the length of one of Greg's hills. Its lack of trees gives it the uncomfortable appearance of a rip in a woman's nylon stocking, exposing the skin beneath, conspicuous in its contrast to the life around it; it would be less awkward if she wore no stockings at all. Knowing the genesis of the barren land—strip mining—evokes a feeling more severe. The sense is that the skin was torn, then left exposed to rot or heal, whichever happened first.

Drive anywhere around Appalachia, and you will see these strips. In 2013, coal was still providing 69 percent of Ohio's electricity, compared with 37 percent nationwide.[18] Strip mining (a type of surface mining) is a method of extracting coal near to the earth's surface. Surface mines are cheaper, faster, and require fewer workers than underground mines, which they began to outnumber in the middle of the twentieth century. One surface mine was active in Carroll County, Ohio, when I visited in 2012, while nearly thirty others powered the state; hundreds more are in disuse.[19] In an active strip mine, the top layers of surface and soil, dispassionately called "overburden," are removed in strips by equipment and explosives, and then moved aside to an already-mined pit. The underlying coal is excavated and moved downstream for processing. The emptied earth is filled up again by the next strip's overburden. Refilling the land is intended as part of a "reclamation" process to allow the earth to grow life again.[20]

That certainly did not happen on Greg's land, or on other hills within my sight. Greg's neighbor John points out that in neighboring Harrison County, where surface mining was even more prevalent, there are "these lovely rolling hills and no trees, no springs. It's all spoiled . . . just beyond imagination." John manages a positive spin: "the best you can do with it is graze it. And then it's going to be nurturing intensive in terms of fertilizer and nutrient application. It's not quite as bad as Colorado, though." Disrupting the composition of the soil, and thus its fertility, creates the most visible damage. Yet coal mines harm more than the land beneath them. Often, they pollute groundwater or divert its flow patterns. Greg points out that because of all the deep mining in nearby Belmont County, the groundwater and wells there are no longer usable and people must consume municipal water instead ("you see lots of fire hydrants"). John points to Colorado, Greg to Belmont County. How comforting is the logic of relativity.

Clearly, the mining companies are not known for their environmentalism. But the one that came to Greg's land took a liking to his trees. When they came to negotiate a lease, they were already privy to the success of Greg's farming and "decided they'd grow chestnut trees too!" So the coal miners were in the chestnut business, at least until they took their coal and left Greg's land.

As it happens, the land in eastern Ohio contains more riches than coal alone. Under the earth are shale rock formations holding oil and gas within their hardened layers. When people stumbled on these formations in Pennsylvania and Ohio, they named them Marcellus and Utica. To liberate their bounty, they developed methods of horizontal drilling and hydraulic fracturing—called "fracking" by all but its spokespeople. The discoveries spurred rave reviews: Staggering Global Potential—Cause for Celebration—Challenges Saudi Reserves—The Next Energy Revolution—Boom Rattles OPEC—U.S. Will Be Self-sufficient! And indeed, shale rock deposits produced more than eleven trillion cubic feet of shale gas in the United States in 2013, up from three thousand in 2009, and *none* in 2006.[21] Gas from shale accounted for 1 percent of domestic gas production in 2000; a decade later, it accounted for 20 percent; by 2035, it may reach 46 percent.[22] But a number of technical issues—most importantly drilling intensity, according to experts—may limit future potential. Nobody really knows how much of the stuff will come out of the ground yet.

Moreover, we don't know the cost of the extraction. I had hoped to find out when I spoke to Ann Harris, a geologist at Youngstown

State University. She wants to be optimistic about the potential of shale, yet she notes, cautiously and repeatedly, "It's all about the geology." Harris thinks its impact on the land will be less dramatic than that of the coal mines she studies. Still, she reminds me of the earthquake that shook downtown Youngstown in January 2012, the eleventh in as many months. It originated from a hydraulic fracturing well.[23] She tells stories of gas coming out of kitchen water faucets in people's homes, and of tap water that develops a top layer of gaseous bubbles after sitting for a few moments. It is almost certain that more long-term environmental consequences will appear, although so far their nature remains obscure.[24] We await the unknown quantities of gas and damage alike.

Greg hopes to find out more about shale's potential soon. Just as a coal company once leased his land, so now does a shale company. His first lease began in 2000. Because that was before the boom, he received just five dollars per acre. "Then the tsunami hit," Greg says.

In 2010, Greg signed a three-year lease with Anschutz Exploration after several calls and visits from one of their "land men." (In an aside, Greg offers up a joke: "How can you tell if a land man is lying? His lips are moving.") This time the company offered him two hundred dollars per acre, per year. Moreover, as a "signing bonus" to contract with the company for three years, he received all the money up front—six hundred dollars per acre. But even that price was dwarfed by more recent boom prices. Beginning in 2011, "lease prices exploded and drilling rigs descended like an alien invasion," Greg recalls. In late 2012, Chesapeake Energy noticed that one acre of Greg's land was not under lease (a small land swap with his neighbor had caused some confusion). So the company made Greg a lease offer—a boom offer—of $5,800 for that single acre. As he signed, he imagined what might have been, had he waited another year instead of signing off on his nearly two hundred acres in 2010.

At the time we spoke, Greg's land was "held by production": a drilling unit from a nearby well has been dug under his land. His lease was set to expire, but while under production he would not be able to renew it or receive any new payments. The expectation is that gas will emerge from that drill, and then Greg will begin to receive royalties at the rate of 14 percent of gross production. At that point, "all of a sudden the signing bonus is pretty small, we hope [*laughs*]. I guess that remains to be seen. If you believe what they tell you [*laughs*]." But we're getting ahead of ourselves.

Royalties represent the last of three phases, as Greg describes them. Leasing was the first. Construction followed, and carries on. It begins with the well pads that feed the horizontal drills stretching out through the layers of rock. From late 2010 to early 2015, nearly two thousand permits were granted for the drilling of wells in the Utica shale in Ohio; 1,348 had already been drilled.[25] The energy companies are building pipelines and processing plants to funnel the energy that is waiting to spew forth. I drove through Carroll County at night and saw well pads lit up, each a miniature Eiffel Tower emblazoned with flood lights; men worked through the night, every night. By day, trucks roam endlessly through the once slow and quiet countryside; residents complain about the influx of trucks and the damage to their roads. Greg says the companies are digging and building "just as fast as they possibly can."

In the meantime, the companies are not particularly communicative—a landowner probably will not know when, where, or if a drill will pass through his land. That is the case with Greg's neighbor John, who tells me, "The site is all prepared, but it's just been sitting. I don't know why. You never know. The company doesn't tell you much." Greg echoes John's sentiment, noting that the energy companies "seem to be really poor about communicating with the leaseholders." But John's not overly concerned with their communication skills—after all, money talks.

"For the local people, it's fantastic!" John exclaims. He proceeds to tell me a series of anecdotes. There was his aging friend with deteriorating health who couldn't afford to retire because his wife was diagnosed with cancer and all the money from his dairy cows went toward their health insurance; with the money from their lease, he won't be milking cows until his dying day, he can afford their health insurance, his wife is healing, and the two have even taken a couple of vacations. Then there is John's son-in-law, who used the proceeds from his lease to buy new farm equipment, "so now he's kind of living the dream, which is how to make a small fortune in farming—you start with a big fortune [*laughs*] and farm until it's gone."

John jests, but he makes a serious point: "It may prolong some of the farming." He continues, "I think the reason that it's hard for young folks to become engaged in [farming] on a full-time basis is because of the economics. It's just so capital intensive that you couldn't afford it. So [energy leases] will provide opportunity, I think, for more young people to become involved, if they choose." All the farmers I spoke to around Ohio made the same point: financially, farming is prohibitive. Might it be possible that the fuel industry will support farming, rather than displace it? If the money from leases and royalties is reinvested in the land, might shale save agriculture?

It's too soon to tell. But Greg ponders these questions endlessly. The critical question to ask about the shale wealth, he tells me, is, "What will people do?"

Not just what they have or what they can buy. But what will they do with their lives? Just subsist off the wealth? Will they live happily if they're not doing something that contributes? My ideal scenario is they take a fraction and put it into agricultural development. Then, we'll still have something to do. And that means making money from it. No matter how environmentally worthy it is, it is only sustainable if it's economically viable. And oil and gas drilling doesn't have any viability. As a society, a county, a family, we have to ask what we are going to do with this one-time lottery winning.

Greg is living by his ideals. He has put money into establishing the chestnut co-op, and lives to watch over the chestnuts, not the oil nor the gas, that come from his land.

He hopes, but cautiously. He points out that other countries with mineral wealth—countries in Africa, for example—are not exactly basking in peace and prosperity. Greg's focus remains on home, though. Since most people in Carroll County are not landowners, they are not all blessed by the bounty of the shale boom. Moreover, given the low level of property taxes in the area (among the lowest rates in Ohio), the money from leases and royalties is not being pumped into public services. The newest school building, he notes, was built in 1959; and "bad schools," he asks, "produce what kind of people?"

Greg turns his clock forward several decades. There, in the wide view of the future, "the mineral extraction becomes a real short-term event." Man will have burnt the hydrocarbons. The chestnuts will remain.

.   .   .

Mineral extraction is indeed a short-term event in history. For tens of thousands of years, solar power fueled the animals and plants that allowed for human activity. It was only about two hundred years ago that we learned how to extract coal from the earth at productive rates, to power our engines with steam, and to produce our iron efficiently. Within a century, oil replaced coal as our most crucial source of energy, fueling our machines and daily lives with even more power and vigor. Just one hundred years after that, we are already forecasting the end of oil, calculating what remains of the reserves we have been burning through rapid-fire. In looking for alternative sources of energy, the most forward-looking solutions appear to revisit the past: the sun and the wind might again power our lives. But we will not abandon our codependent relationship with fossil fuels until absolutely necessary—and any sign of its health draws us back in like giddy addicts. Hence the excitement over shale: the rocks promise new stores of oil and gas. More exciting yet, they are here, in America, below our feet, so we may declare energy independence from turbaned sheikhs and other foreign elements! Our unbridled excitement over the prospect of energy independence (free markets and globalization to the wind) is as good an indication as any of our dependence on energy.

Many Americans do not realize that our most basic human activity—eating—is now fully dependent on the burning of spectacular amounts of fossil fuel, at least as dependent on it as our transportation. The food industrial complex, as some observers call it, is where Dave's corn and Greg's gas meet, fuel each other, and keep Americans hungry for more.

Investigating the agricultural industry, writer Michael Pollan traces the historical development of the relationship between food and fossil fuels. The supply of corn in America far exceeds consumer demand—its production does not follow the logic of that straightforward market model. Rather, corn has become a "commodity grain," valued for the quantity produced regardless of market conditions. The federal government, not the American consumer, is paying "nearly half the income of the average Iowa corn farmer."[26] This model keeps production high and prices low, so farmers grow ever more corn to maintain their incomes, driving prices lower still. That leaves us with "mountains of cheap corn." An industrial food system steps in to move the mountains.

Agribusiness corporations are primed to correct (and maintain) the imbalance in the corn market. Take Cargill, for example, the biggest private company in the United States, which brought in $1.49 trillion in revenue in 2012.[27] According to Pollan, Cargill and another company, ADM, broker the entire corn cycle:

> They provide the pesticide and fertilizer to the farmers; operate most of America's grain elevators; broker and ship most of the exports; perform the wet and dry milling; feed the livestock and then slaughter the corn-fattened animals; distill the ethanol; and manufacture the high-fructose corn syrup and the numberless other fractions derived from field corn. Oh yes—and help write many of the rules that govern this whole game.[28]

The results of this massive enterprise? We've reconfigured the digestive systems of cows to ingest corn instead of grass, and more than a quarter of the items in the American supermarket now contain corn. One soft drink, consisting almost entirely of high-fructose corn syrup, is made from a third of a pound of corn; a four-ounce burger, from two pounds of corn; and so on. Corn in all its forms is our cheapest and most abundant source of calories.

And if corn is fueling us, what is fueling corn? Enter oil. It began with fertilizer. Once upon a time, the sun fed the plants, the plants fed the livestock, and the livestock's manure fed the plants again. But then man learned to use fossil fuels to fix nitrogen and create fertilizer, breaking the natural cycle and replacing it with a neat package that could be bought and sold in bulk to allow for the industrial production of corn. Then follow the next steps: use fossil fuels to make pesticides, power the tractors, and transport the corn, and you will have used about fifty gallons of oil per acre of corn.[29] Indeed, one-fifth of our country's petroleum consumption is dedicated to the production and transport of food.[30] That is about equivalent to the amount of petroleum consumed by our cars.

If the shale in Greg's land and across Ohio and Pennsylvania unlocks significant amounts of gas, energy will remain affordable for longer. That will let a farmer like Dave sell his corn to agribusiness corporations that will ensure our food stays cheaper for longer too. Daniel's fruits and vegetables, meanwhile, just don't factor into this story.

CHAPTER SEVEN

In America, You Pay for Your Teeth

Healthy citizens are the greatest asset any country
can have.
   —Winston Churchill

I fell behind in my house payments because of my surgery. I got a notice from the bank saying I had ninety days to get caught up. I was four months behind. This was January 2009. Before that, I'd been in a group called the Toledo Foreclosure Defense League. We were looking for someone who'd want us to help them defend their home. People were too afraid when we did find them, though. Most of them, when they got the foreclosure notice, they were ready to move out immediately. So we decided to do what we were asking other people to do with my house. I figured I was going to lose it—let's make it worth it, take a stand and send a message.

We spent a long time coming up with different ways to barricade . . . Boarding up windows, putting cement blocks in front of the doorways, setting up computers and even a spy cam . . . we wanted to document how the cops acted when they came in. But we had enough publicity and everything else, that I think we had deterred any kind of police violence when they made an entrance. We live-streamed online. There were seven of us inside. We had a generator because we figured they might pull the electricity and that kind of stuff. We had cords running to the outside;

that's how we got supplies. We were in there for five days. There were plans that day to have a rally there at the house. There were people talking about digging a moat across the driveway. There were people camping out. So, on the fifth day, the swat team broke into the house. We had to be carried out, we wouldn't just go willingly, so we went limp on them. We wanted to make it not easy for them to kick us out.

We had one demand we wanted—to declare a moratorium on foreclosures in Wood County, or they were going to have to drag us out. We had no expectations they were going to cave in, but we wanted to show that the threat of eviction was making people move out when they were getting foreclosures. It never got picked up. There were a couple things here and there that didn't quite go as we had planned . . . we did some other interviews . . . we sat on a couple of panels and activist cooperation. We wanted to spark people into defending their homes. It didn't quite turn out to be the upheaval we were hoping, of resistance.

—Keith, 56, Toledo

Revolution was truant.

.   .   .

Dawn grew up in the 1960s, but a snapshot of her childhood may well reflect an earlier era. That is because her family—settled in a southeastern exurb of Cleveland—was among the working poor. They depended on a cistern for water; they enjoyed it when it rained, and when it didn't, "we didn't have water," she recalls. Her mother would heat the rainwater on the stove, "and all the kids would hurry up and take a bath in the same water before it got cold." Dawn walked across the train tracks to go to school. On days her mother didn't pack her a lunch, she cleaned the counters and tables in the cafeteria—she had cut a deal with the cafeteria ladies: scrubbing for food. When the scrawny brunette sat down to eat that "free" lunch, she digested a life lesson: "Well, if I work hard I can get food! Isn't that great?" And so she worked.

In high school, Dawn discovered herself to be "kind of a bright kid." She enjoyed learning and was good at it. By senior year, she was determined to go to college. Her parents couldn't afford to send her, and at that point they were both descending into alcoholism. So Dawn needed to make enough money to move out of their toxic household and to pay tuition. While still in high school, she assisted in a dentist's office after class, before serving on a night shift at a local restaurant. After graduating, she became a live-in nanny for a stint. By the time she was nineteen, she had saved enough money to move into her own apartment and buy a car. She registered for evening classes at Cuyahoga Community College (Tri-C) and continued working at the dentist's office during the day. "I did that all by myself. I had no help from anybody," Dawn reflects proudly. "And that's pretty great when you think about it."

Then her smile retreats. "Today, I don't think a nineteen-year-old could do that, because it's so different now. I recognize that."

At the same time that she was establishing her financial independence, Dawn was falling in love. Dave grew up one school district over from Dawn. She took him as her date to senior prom. The two parted ways to go to college, he enrolling at Ohio University in southeastern Ohio while she stayed at Tri-C. But for his sophomore year, Dave came back to northeastern Ohio and transferred into Kent State University. By their junior year, in 1973, Dawn and Dave were married. Work and family ensued.

After college, Dave started a career in factory management. The girl from the wrong side of the tracks was laying the foundations for a comfortable life. First, Dawn studied to become a licensed practical nurse. She spent a decade as an orthopedic nurse, before pursuing work in technical medical consulting. Dawn traversed the country, training other nurses in software programs, before partaking in a multihospital study of Cleveland's emergency rooms. She wanted to learn and expand her horizons further, so she returned to school to earn a degree in microcomputer applications. Her own dynamism surprised her.

At the same time that Dawn was advancing her career, she and Dave were making a family. They had two children, a boy and a girl. Their son and his wife have given them two grandchildren; Dawn is hoping their daughter and her husband will do the same. She likes to think she raised her children well. "We were good providers . . . they always had plenty of food and clothing and toys. But I always said to them there is a difference between a need and a want." In the early 1980s, Dave's company transferred him to Florida for nearly eight years. Dawn hated it for a simple reason: "no family." Her parents and Dave's were still up in Ohio. In time, the couple moved back with the kids in tow and bought a home a couple of miles from where they had grown up.

The decade that followed was a nightmare.

In 1994, at the age of forty-one, Dawn was diagnosed with aggressive breast cancer. She underwent a partial mastectomy, followed by chemotherapy and radiation. Two years later, she relapsed. The doctors removed one of her breasts completely. Dawn "just wanted to look normal," so she had reconstructive surgery. Four months later, her doctor saw a spot on her lung. It seemed to be enlarging, and he was sure her cancer was the culprit. The operating table was still warm when Dawn returned to have part of her lung removed. That was "the worst surgery" she had had up to that point. In total, she underwent nine surgeries.

Meanwhile, Dawn's and Dave's parents were dying, one after another, from cancer. Dawn's father died in 1996, followed by Dave's mother in 1997 and then Dawn's mom in 1998. During those turbulent years, Dawn's daughter began to show signs of the upheaval at home, acting out at school. "She was really at a sensitive age when I had cancer; it was really rough on her," Dawn recalls. What happened next shall hardly come as a surprise—Dawn began to suffer from depression.

There, Dawn's insurance company drew the line. The company decided that Dawn had reached a "lifetime limit" on her medical coverage. The termination of coverage left the couple with little choice—they declared bankruptcy. The only bills they needed to write off were medical; neither Dawn nor Dave had credit cards. "We don't use credit cards; if we can't afford something, we don't buy it." The episode embittered Dawn. "Nobody should have to declare bankruptcy or die," she cries. But that is the dilemma she faced and the decision she made.

Dawn's story struck me as especially tragic. But, in fact, it is hardly unique. A 2009 study published in the *American Journal of Medicine* found that the majority of bankruptcies filed in America were attributable to medical costs. Moreover, the proportion of such filings was increasing. In 1981, just 8 percent of families filed bankruptcy as a result of medical costs. Twenty years later, about half of bankruptcies resulted from such costs, and by 2007, medical costs were causing more than 60 percent of bankruptcies. More surprising still, most of the people in these cases, like Dawn, were well-educated homeowners with middle-class occupations. One more stunner: three-quarters of them had health insurance.[1] Nevertheless, an experience shared is not a pain alleviated. The bankruptcy episode hardly helped Dawn's depression. For the time being at least, the couple restructured their finances.

Yet just as Dawn was recovering from her cancer, Dave became ill. In 2006, at the age of fifty-two, he was diagnosed with colorectal cancer. The doctors removed the cancer surgically, and he was spared chemotherapy and radiation. Now Dave was also a cancer survivor. Despite the hopeful connotations of that term, the reality was hardly inspiring: by 2011, the cost of Dave's and Dawn's medical insurance was around $2,500 per month. That was "out of pocket, just the base." There also were the co-pays, the deductibles, and whatever the insurance companies "just arbitrarily didn't pay." They struggled to keep up. Medications became optional; food consumption dwindled to a bare minimum. But sometimes, ends just don't meet. Dawn and Dave missed a mortgage payment.

There was a time, Dawn recalls, when a borrower could call the bank and say, "Hey bank, we have high bills. Can we tack this month's payment onto next month's bill?" Times have changed. "Now, there is no leeway whatsoever. If you pay a day late, a minute late, a second late, they put you right into foreclosure!" And that's exactly what happened. To fend off the foreclosure, Dawn and Dave scrambled together "the extortion money." One way of doing so was suspending their medical coverage, their biggest bill. They saved the house, at least.

Dawn's not entirely sure how they are going to manage in the future without any retirement savings. Having saved their home and health is a less comforting thought than it ought to be. But Dawn's mind isn't on her own troubles anymore.

Misfortune produced in Dawn a powerful transformation: she became politicized. For most of her adulthood, voting marked the extent of her political involvement. Between children and her career, life was just too busy for anything more. But as soon as she stopped working in 2004, Dawn began reading steadily. She consumed books voraciously, finding biographies of presidents especially captivating. She joined a history book club, followed political blogs online, and learned her way around the issues. Discovering that her experiences with banks and health insurance companies were widely shared by others, she realized that the stakes were high for everybody. In 2010, she decided to volunteer for a congressional campaign. In 2012, she became a local leader in the MoveOn progressive action movement. During that year's national election season, Dawn could be found behind the mouthpiece of a megaphone, rallying people to volunteer and to vote for the Democratic Party. Even her personal conversations now included statements like, "There's nothing free about the free market," and "Wall Street is a Las Vegas gambling casino!" Dawn turned her suffering into activism.

My second meeting with Dawn took place almost a year after Barack Obama was reelected to the presidency. She was grateful, if only for his healthcare policy. But she was also moving on to other political causes. Dawn had found feminism. She had not yet figured out how she would pursue this new passion, but one thing was clear: she looked healthy.

. . .

Loraine wishes she could fight off foreclosures, but not to save her own home. She wants to save her neighborhood. The City of Lorain, in northern Ohio, sits on Lake Erie, with the water every bit a part of the town's character. After marrying an American and emigrating from England in the early 1970s, Loraine adopted Lorain as her own—so much so that she now directs her neighborhood's historical preservation society. The shared namesake of town and lady is serendipity.

Loraine's husband found himself in Lorain by accident. He is from Sandusky, further west. Upon completing service in the U.S. Air Force, he returned home and hopped on a bus to Cleveland, hoping to find work in the big city. The bus broke down, and, while waiting for another to come along, he flipped through the phone book and found a company called Lorain Products, "which was into electronics." He called them up, was offered a job, and stayed in Lorain. Some years later, at a pub in London, England, he fell into conversation with a local woman. She noticed his perfect teeth and assumed he was wealthy, "because you have to pay for your teeth in America." Eventually, she found out that he was not, in fact, rich, but "by then it was too late." Loraine was already home in Lorain.

The couple's American house might well have been transported from the English countryside. The Tudor-style home features white stucco panels crisscrossed with dark brown timber, crowned with steeply pitched roofing. Groomed bushes and flowers fill every inch of the front yard, from which ivy crawls up the façade of the house and nearly covers two plaques by the main door: one with the street address, the other bearing the house's name. Naming one's house is an English tradition, I am told.

Loraine's attention to detail is visible throughout the neighborhood. Her son, an artist, painted the street signs around the town's few blocks. "He did a lot of community work for me because he had to. I told him he had to," she recalls proudly. Back in the 1980s, Loraine and two other residents in the neighborhood founded the

Charleston Village Society. They petitioned to have the neighborhood, the oldest in Lorain, designated "historic" by the city and since then have focused on preservation. Their efforts have included restoring park areas, creating a tribute site for a U.S. Navy Fleet commander from Lorain, and recruiting local artists to carve old tree trunks into sculptures. At the time we met, Loraine was engaged in a project to create a "Hero's Walk" on unclaimed land to honor the members of the community who died in Iraq and Afghanistan.

One might forgive Loraine, then, for feeling that blight has infected her community.

She admits that the community's housing problems predate the recession, pointing to a house on the corner that has been empty for forty years. Local government officials, no matter what their political affiliation, have never taken her complaints about the abandoned house seriously. That lack of response by the local administration persists, so Loraine's self-described "nagging" has not let up either. But there was a time when that empty corner house was the exception, not the rule. Through the years, the character of the community has changed—in Loraine's opinion, for the worse.

It began with the busing. Until the 1990s, Loraine felt that hers was a good middle-class neighborhood with a pretty decent school just across the street from her home. "But then they decided to ruin that and make busing the mandatory thing." She catches her transgression of political correctness and continues, "We didn't need it in Lorain; this community was desegregated already." Next thing she knew, her daughter was coming home from school in tears, while her son was getting pushed around in the schoolyard. The changes would not push Loraine out—she liked her house and the nearby lake too much. Instead, she pulled her kids out of the public school system and enrolled them in Catholic school. Some years later, the public school closed. The student body had been shrinking, and the city decided to concentrate students in other area schools. The school building was converted into a warehouse before being sold to a charter school.

When Loraine looks at homes, including her own, she sees more than dollar signs. For her, community and history are built into the foundation of every house. Still, like a well-adjusted American, she sees investment value too. And as Loraine walks us through the evolution of her neighborhood, we would be amiss not to address the rise in real estate values in America from the late 1990s to the mid-2000s, and the devastating decline that followed. True, the city of Lorain is no Las Vegas; it was not a hot spot for flipping condos in those years (or ever, for that matter). Still, the overall housing index in Cleveland, just thirty miles from Lorain, *did* rise just as steadily, if not as steeply, as prices in the rest of the country during that period. The nature of the expanding housing bubble is critical to our understanding of the eventual bust and its aftermath.

For more than a century, housing prices in America rose at a re-markably stable rate. From 1890 to 1997, national real estate prices grew by 9 percent in real terms. In the decade that followed, values suddenly skyrocketed: house prices rose by 79 percent between 1997 and 2006.[2] Many Americans came to believe emphatically that a house could serve as a highly profitable investment: buy now, sell later, and pocket a great return. Not everybody was buying houses just to flip them. Still, most believed that a house was the best place to hold and buttress one's wealth. Presumably, professional financiers should have known that the growing supply in houses would necessarily bring down prices; they also should have considered the consequences of artificially low and unsustainable mortgage rates. Instead, many of them were making the same bets as the homebuyers.[3]

An enthusiastic government helped catalyze the rapid rise in real estate values. Following the 2001 recession, the Federal Reserve lowered interest rates to encourage consumer borrowing. During his tenure, President George W. Bush was driven by his vision for an "ownership society." In 2004, he credited his policies for a rise in the rate of home ownership to an all-time high, adding that he hoped to oversee further growth through the supply of millions of more affordable homes, "so more American families will be able to open the door and say 'Welcome to my home.'"[4] Specifically, he pursued policies for increasing home ownership among minorities. The low interest rates and other policy initiatives worked too well. Banks were offering mortgages with historically low interest rates to borrowers who would have been unlikely to have afforded them—or qualified for them—in the past. In the mid-1990s, about 65 percent of Americans owned their homes; one decade later, nearly seven in ten Americans were homeowners. Rates of ownership among minorities increased apace.

Everyone seemed pleased that more Americans were buying their homes: home ownership is a part of the American Dream, after all. And it does have a certain "feel good" effect on one's sense of financial stability. Moreover, there are important political and social consequences of homeownership, including a greater commitment to the local community and a higher likelihood of voting. That home ownership actually has few inherent advantages for the overall economy is less important in this national narrative.

The American Dream aside, accessible subprime mortgage lending was bringing people into Loraine's neighborhood that she didn't care for. Loraine may or may not have been especially discomforted by the rise in the black population there. She never said so explicitly. But this discussion about housing is an opportunity to note that, with or without subprime lending, rates of home ownership in America are significantly lower among blacks than among the general population. While in 1995, 70 percent of whites owned their homes, just 42 percent of blacks were homeowners. In the early 2000s, black ownership of homes climbed to nearly 50 percent, before falling again after the recession.[5]

Regardless of her ambivalence toward her new neighbors, Loraine couldn't have foreseen the true blight that was coming to the entire country. The ceaseless supply of new houses, the aggressive promotion of subprime mortgages, the low interest rates, and the "irrationally exuberant" trading of bundled mortgages on Wall Street—none of it could last.[6] Pop went the housing bubble. From their peak in 2006, home prices had plummeted by 33 percent by the time they bottomed out in 2009.

Bad loans came to haunt those involved. In February 2007, the U.S. chief of the British bank HSBC resigned because his customers weren't paying back their loans. In April, New Century Financial, forced to repurchase its own bad loans, filed for bankruptcy. The next month, USB closed down its subprime arm. In August, Ameriquest— the largest of the subprime lenders—went out of business.[7] By year's end, twenty-five subprime lenders had declared bankruptcy.

And it only got worse.

In 2008, the housing crisis brought the major banks on Wall Street to their knees. There, bankers had been enthusiastically buying and selling mortgage-backed securities (bundled mortgages) from lending institutions, including those of the subprime variety. When borrowers began to default on their mortgages and the lending institutions suffered, the banks holding the securities lost big. In March 2008, bad loans brought down Bear Sterns, a global bank trading in securities, and others were set to follow. As the financial system began to collapse, the federal government padded the fall with hundreds of billions of dollars.

Back in Lorain and across the country, the latest wave in the economic tsunami—the foreclosure crisis—was forcing people out of their homes. Suffering the reverberations of the housing bust and the onset of the Great Recession, many Americans were failing to make their house payments. Some were unable to pay because of job losses; others were reluctant to continue making mortgage payments on homes that were losing value every day. With Wall Street in a tumult, credit ceased to flow between banks and consumers just when they needed it most. Still other homeowners became the victims of fraudulent and erroneous foreclosures. Back in 2004, Lorain County had experienced 1,500 foreclosure cases. In 2009, nearly 2,700 foreclosures were filed. That same year, more than 89,000 foreclosures were filed across the state of Ohio, 30,000 more than in 2004.[8] Between 2007 and 2012, the United States witnessed 4 million foreclosures.

Loraine didn't like this. She feels a great deal of dismay for regular homeowners. In her opinion, the banks are primarily to blame for the community disturbance, which was aggravated by predatory home-buyers scooping up foreclosed homes. Together, the banks and the landlords "prostitute these houses." She paints a grim image by way of example: The historic parsonage down the street sold for $75,000 dollars in 2006; after reclaiming it, the bank sold it for $11,000. And the blue house just next door? After once being sold for $60,000, it was foreclosed on in 2008 and has been sitting empty since then. The city bought it with money provided by a federal neighborhood stabiliza-tion program, only to have a bank buy it for $38,000 at the sheriff's auction and then dump it back on the market for just $10,000.[9] The people buying houses at these low prices weren't families in need of homes; instead, they were cash-paying landlords and property rental groups eagerly grasping at the cheap real estate.

For Loraine, such trends threaten more than house prices—com-munal life is at stake. When a landlord buys up ten properties, his influence on the neighborhood is disproportionate to that of a single homeowner like Loraine. Local control over the neighborhood is lost to managers lacking personal investment in the upkeep of houses they do not live in themselves. "Who is going to determine the condition of the neighborhood?" Loraine asks rhetorically. "Me, with my one little property? Or the guy that owns eight houses on the block?" The related problem is that these landlords are renting cheaply to individuals Loraine deems "questionable." She finds confirmation for her fears in her own research. Each time there is a crime in the neighborhood, she tells me, "I look it up and it's a renting tenant from one of these landlords." The new residents are "becoming a glut in this community," she moans.

The worse it gets, the less likely it becomes that Loraine's ideal neighbors will move in and that she will ever again live in the type of American community she entered forty years ago. Still, she will not cease in her efforts to improve the neighborhood. She may have arrived here through the accident of a broken-down bus and a miscalculation about nice teeth, but Lorain is ever Loraine's home.

. . .

Paula and Billy were married for almost thirty years before they purchased their own home. Paula grew up in Frankfurt, a small rural town in south-central Ohio. Billy is from the eastern Indiana countryside. When he was nineteen years old, Billy worked on a construction project in Ohio tasked with installing a water line through Frankfurt. Each day, the crew went for lunch at the diner where eighteen-year-old Paula had become a waitress after graduating from high school. Their short lunchtime encounters became meetings after work, and soon enough the courtship acquired the sanction of marriage. When the water line was complete, Paula packed up her bags and left the only town she knew, heading west toward Indiana.

The young couple moved in with Billy's parents and worked on the family farm. They had a son and a daughter. Paula describes those years:

> We would work in tobacco because that's what his family did. Him and I would both go down and take the two kids with us and work in the tobacco. We'd put them in the walker or playpen and work. We lived off the farm. I washed clothes by hand, go down to the creek and get a bucket of water. We were hillbillies. It wasn't that long ago, but it seems like another world, how rough it was.

Physical exertion on the farm failed to translate into economic comfort. Paula and Billy felt their poverty in their backs and bones. Job prospects off the farm were grim—deindustrialization seemed to be corroding the whole state of Indiana in the 1980s. Five years in, Paula received a promising phone call from her father. He told her that a landowner in Bainbridge, about thirty miles south of Paula's hometown of Frankfurt, was looking for a caretaker for his farm; he was willing to house the couple and their children in a small cottage on the land. Paula took her husband and children back home to Ohio.

To supplement his new work on the farm, Billy began driving log trucks full-time. Even so, the couple recognized that they needed another income. Paula waited until the kids—by now there was a third—were in school, and enrolled in college courses in accounting and legal secretarial training. "I got as many degrees as I could for the time that I was there to have more of a variety," she explains. Her approach paid off. Within a week of graduating, a certified public accounting (CPA) firm in Chillicothe called Paula and requested her résumé. She was hired as a secretary in 1996, and has worked for the same firm ever since.

During my conversation with the couple, Paula did most of the talking. Billy was quiet, perhaps hesitant about my presence at his kitchen table. Given his rugged looks—arms and torso thick from years of physical labor—one might not expect Billy's bashfulness. When I asked him to describe his background, though, he offered only these few words: "I'm just from Indiana, there's nothing to tell."

But as the evening proceeded and Paula filled in the blanks for her husband, Billy became less reticent. He works sixty-five hours per week driving the truck, and forty to fifty hours per month on the farm, depending on the season, he tells me. "My hours are daylight to dark, [laughs] dark to dark. I leave here about 4:30, get home maybe 6, maybe 8." I ask him if he likes what he does.

BILLY: I really don't have a choice. I'd rather do something easier, or just work one job.
PAULA: He likes it.
BILLY: Yeah, but it's getting harder and harder.
PAULA: He loves the farm.
BILLY: Oh yeah. And I growed up around the trucks, it's in my blood. I started pulling a tanker when I was sixteen years

old. You're only allowed to drive eleven hours now—they changed the law—and there's got to be a break in there. I listen to the radio, and I smoke while I'm driving. I used to drive a thousand miles a day, never did bother me. Now it's about six- or seven-hundred-mile days. . . . On the farm, I do whatever the need. Mowing, weeding, trimming, whatever has to be done. Basically, I'm on twenty-four-hour call. I love that farm there because I love fooling with the cows, raising the horses, watching the corn grow. But it's a stressful job, farming. If you're supposed to be mowing but it's raining, then I'll go clean the barns out. It has to be do-ed [done]. You got to do it.

Paula worries about Billy out on the roads. She laments that trucking is "very dangerous"; Billy disagrees. In a tone expressing both admiration and concern, Paula describes her husband as a workaholic. On this count, he concurs. "It's the way I was raised, I guess." Growing up on the farm, Billy helped his mother milk the cows every morning before school; after school, he stripped tobacco until bedtime. "Became part of my nature. It took the family to run the farms back then, 'cause you couldn't afford to hire anybody."

Unlike Billy, Paula allows herself the occasional vacation. She used to take the kids on trips with her mother or sister while he stayed behind, too concerned about the farm to leave it. But as much as she did for them, Paula always wishes that she could have been more involved with the kids as they were growing up. Work at the accounting firm is intense; around tax season, she finds herself in the office six days per week. Paula first entered the labor force to help provide her family with additional income. In time, though, her salary came to exceed her husband's. Altogether they make less than sixty thousand dollars per year.

For all these years, Billy and Paula worked tirelessly. They endured the work, the "violence to their bodies and their spirits," as Studs Terkel would have told it.[10] The payoff?

Not a dime in savings.

Nearly thirty years into marriage, Paula and Billy bought their first home. For a time after her father's phone call beckoned the couple back from Indiana, they lived in the cottage on the farm Billy cared for. However, with three children prompting a need for more space, they soon rented a house on another farm just up the hill. They rented that home for twenty years, with no plans to leave. Then the owner passed away, and the new proprietor decided to turn the house into his hunting cabin. Paula and Billy were unprepared. Again displaying his magnanimity, the farm owner employing Billy purchased a house up for auction. Paula and Billy got their finances in order, took out a loan, and bought the house from him. "We definitely love them," Paula says of the landowner and his wife. "They've been there since day one. We're family," she says, beaming.

At present, the mortgage, $650 per month, is their biggest expense. Their adult children take second place. Of Paula and Billy's three children—one son and two daughters, all in their twenties— none went to college. One is married; they all have children. "We've always helped our kids," Paula begins. "We would be in better shape if we didn't have to [*laughs*], a lot better shape with our retirement savings, because now there is none [*laughs*]."

Their son, the eldest child, lives with his parents. Things were going fine for him until the economic downturn. He was laid off from his manufacturing job in 2010. Married at the time, he and his wife immediately faced financial difficulties that ended in bankruptcy; the divorce filing followed not long after. Soon enough, he moved in with his parents, joined by his two children on weekends. At the time of our meeting, he was back at work. But with two children to support, it seemed he would be living with his parents for a while yet.

Although the girls don't live with Paula and Billy, they also receive their support. The older daughter works as a manager at a local fast-food joint. She lives with her boyfriend, who stays at home with their child. Her full-time job brings in only twelve thousand dollars per year. "She makes week-to-week, check-to-check, barely," her mother laments, "so we help out as much as we can whenever she needs it." The roles are reversed in the home of the youngest daughter. She stays at home with her two children, while her husband works as a welder. She has some ambition to get a degree and work ("I'm thinking she's wanting to go into secretarial"), but any job she might get with her high-school education would be unlikely to cover the cost of putting the kids in day care.

Paula and Billy recognize the incongruence of caring for their adult children instead of preparing for their retirement. Paula never thought it would be this way; she dreamed of her children, each in turn, getting married, moving out, and making a living, the way her generation did. "I think everybody's just lazy!" Billy chimes in. "They don't want to work." Billy offers an example (by now all too familiar) of a young man he hired to help on the farm, who gave up because the work was too hard. His own son, he admits, runs away from chores and certainly would not work two jobs, as Billy does. Paula is not above self-recrimination. "Maybe we make it too easy for them to have an out. We always want to make sure our kids have things that we didn't have—have it easier. Maybe if they could have had a rougher time . . ." But she articulates some of the structural elements at play too: "It's not just our family with non-college education. Everyone I see in different income levels, the kids are still—You know, costs are so high; everything costs. I don't think our income has gone up enough to make it even. Things are surpassing wages." Billy nods in agreement. The fuel in his truck costs three times what it used to, he notes.

One of the most worrying aspects of this situation is Billy's lack of healthcare coverage. Paula and the children are all insured, she and her son through their employers, the girls through Medicaid. Only Billy lacked coverage. Well, he and the forty-eight million other Americans without insurance in 2012. Like fifteen million of those people, it didn't matter that he worked full-time, year-round.[11] Billy acknowledges the problem but also fails to do anything about it. He has never had health coverage and can't remember the last time he saw a doctor; he's not particularly eager to visit one. "They just tell you stuff you don't want to hear," he explains. When we spoke, Paula and Billy were debating whether they would purchase him individual health insurance in late 2013, as mandated by President Obama's Affordable Care Act. If rates remain high, they reasoned, they might just pay the fee for noncompliance instead. After all, the high premiums on private insurance for a male smoker in his fifties have held them back until now. That's right: Billy smokes up to a pack of cigarettes per day.

.   .   .

Dawn, Paula, and their husbands did things "right." They worked hard, produced nuclear families, and lived moderately and modestly. Yet they have no savings to their names. Looking toward the years ahead, these couples see much less stability and fewer rewards for their hard work than they had ever expected.

Failing to save seems as American as apple pie. But the trend to spend has increased considerably over the last few decades. During the 1970s, Americans saved, on average, more than 8 percent of their disposable incomes. Saving declined through the 1980s, so that average savings had fallen below 6 percent of disposable income by the 1990s and declined further, to less than 4 percent of disposable income, in the early 2000s. Savings finally bottomed out at a low of less than 2 percent of disposable income in 2005, before people began to save a little more again after the economic crisis. Economist Jeffrey Sachs worries about such low savings rates, because saving is exactly the "self-control needed for a household's sustained well-being." He writes that in the thirty years preceding the recession, "the nation as a whole, through countless individual decisions of households, lost the self-discipline to save for the future."[12] But Sachs doesn't explain why this occurred.

Like anything else, the trend is the result of several causes. One primary factor is our consumerist culture. Another is the disparity between wages and the costs of living. In Cleveland, for example, the median household income for married-couple families is just under fifty thousand dollars per year; at the same time, "basic household costs" (including housing, food, transportation, childcare, and taxes) exceed sixty thousand dollars.[13] These costs have grown faster than incomes through the years. Between 1990 and 2008, housing prices increased by 56 percent (in inflation-adjusted terms); health care, by a staggering 155 percent; and public college, by 60 percent. Meanwhile, incomes have risen by only 20 percent.[14] Little wonder it's difficult to balance the books when costs are so heavy.

A spending mentality would make it still harder to save. When writing about Americans' failure to save, Sachs uses indeterminate terms like "self-discipline" and "self-control." While such normative concepts might be pertinent, they reveal little about underlying causes and mechanisms. Poor long-term planning may have a more tangible explanation.

Economist Sendhil Mullainathan and psychologist Eldar Shafir sought to uncover the determinants of self-discipline, or the lack thereof, among people with scarce means. They found that when people are in situations of scarcity their cognitive ability is impeded. This, in turn, impairs their decision making about the future, often deepening the initial scarcity. Although their work focuses on poverty, Mullainathan and Shafir's scarcity framework allows for a wide range of contexts. Scarcity applies to a persistently poor family just as it does to the limited time of an overcommitted academic or to an unexpected monetary squeeze on an otherwise comfortable household. In all cases, when our attention is captured by immediate scarcity, we have fewer mental resources to apply to planning ahead.[15]

People who are a little less than comfortable can still fare pretty well from day to day. Mullainathan and Shafir find that people of limited monetary means are actually as good or better than richer people in meeting daily and pressing financial needs. The money spent at a grocery store means more to those with less, so they pay closer attention to exactly how they spend it. On the other hand, poorer people may fare less well when it comes to long-term financial planning, like borrowing and saving, because so much of their cognitive ability is engaged with getting by in the present. Mullainathan and Shafir (together with other researchers) conclude that in our financial lives, "preoccupations with pressing budgetary concerns leave fewer cognitive resources available to guide choice and action."[16] Understanding the science of scarcity turns out to be a rather enlightening endeavor.

The impact of scarcity on cognitive ability might help us understand why some of the people in these pages find themselves without savings. They usually get by, even during the most pressing of times: when Dawn faced foreclosure, for example, she and her husband "scraped together" the money needed to avoid it, while Paula and Billy similarly managed to afford a mortgage despite having no prior plans to leave their rented house. More importantly, both families lived for years in comfortable homes, fed their children well, gave them gifts on birthdays and holidays, and maintained decent standards of living. But only for the moment in which they were living.

Interestingly, both of these couples shared an aversion to credit cards. They never used them, explaining that they didn't want to spend money they didn't have. Such a decision actually reflects a good deal of self-discipline. Yet it may also reflect an inability to deal with future finances. Families with higher incomes are certainly not irresponsible for using credit cards, but that's because they know they will be able to make their payments.

While poorer families focus on their daily bread, other aspects of life slide away. Dawn explicitly acknowledged that her daughter had problems in school during her illness. Paula regrets that she and Billy failed to save enough to help their children go to college. In fact, none of the children in these two families attended college. That fact is especially surprising in Dawn's case: she and her husband both have graduate degrees. But in terms of the model of the American Dream, even Paula and Billy's kids would be expected to exceed the accomplishments of their parents; instead, they are worse off and might remain so. Yes, there just wasn't a lot of money to put away. But, just as importantly, mental resources might have been too stretched.

The implications of such stories are personal *and* political. For much of her adult life, Dawn never had time to read, let alone become politically active, because in the moments that she wasn't working, raising children, and battling cancer, she was fighting off bankruptcy and foreclosure. Paula stopped attending church long ago; working on Saturdays meant that Sunday was her only day to catch up on chores at the house. When Billy has a precious moment of downtime, he just wants to open a can of beer and watch some TV. Who can blame him? Yet such withdrawals from political and community involvement mean that in trying to stay afloat, people such as these are not engaging as full-time citizens.

CHAPTER EIGHT

So Goes the Nation

At some point in each of these stories, government and society intersect. From disability and unemployment assistance to crop and corporate subsidies, people are affected every day by policy and policy makers. I happened to speak with many of my interviewees during a particularly political period: the 2012 electoral campaign season. But I have tried to avoid writing a book about partisan politics, even if it is about a swing state. Mainstream political discourse spews forth enough on that topic already. To engage in the superficial and polarizing terms used by politicians and pundits would diminish the complexity of lived experiences.

Indeed, it often seems that mainstream political discourse diverts attention from everyday economic struggles, emphasizing instead important but exaggerated social divisions. Even when economic issues are discussed, the conversations tend to be hollow. For instance, the 2012 presidential candidates regularly invoked the "middle class," an undefined group of people whose post-recession plight was a declared priority. Yet I frequently found that this middle class would not have included a number of my interviewees who self-identified as members of that group. Many of these interviewees based their sense of belonging to the middle class on the surprisingly low criterion of not requiring government assistance—a line they not infrequently traversed in both directions. Considering the Right's explicit denunciations of social welfare since the Reagan era, its members' conception of the middle class surely would not encompass these people, who occasionally benefit from such assistance. As for the Democrats, they have seemed too enfeebled by the predominant discourse (or by their reliance on affluent campaign contributors) to vocalize or draw attention to their policies, which do encompass social support for such people. All the while, Americans in deeper poverty, whose ranks widened considerably during the Great Recession, were invariably ignored.

Even if we accept that policy makers care genuinely about average Americans, their performance in government at the time of writing has failed to deliver, and partisan conflict prevails in Washington. From his farm in southeastern Ohio, Dave complained, "It's almost like Washington is a different world. They fight, never get anything done, and it's only going to get worse." I suspect many share his sentiments. Though his electoral victories were decisive, the country seems to have fractured further during Barack Obama's presidency. In October 2013, the U.S. government closed its doors, literally paralyzed by partisanship. Such disagreements are not entirely new. The federal government has partly or completely shut down seventeen times since the 1970s because of budget disputes over social welfare policies and such issues as abortion, health care, support for public works, and government spending generally.[1] The more distant past was hardly more harmonious. Just consider the historical experiences of women, leftists, industrial workers, Mormons, Jews, Japanese Americans, Irish Americans, and African slaves. Societal divisions, even if particularly pitched, will always be part of our political lives.

There is another reality that demands attention at this moment in history. It could also lend itself to a discourse of two Americas, but the relevant division is not red and blue. Income inequality has reached historically high levels in the United States, and there is no indication that this trend will slow or reverse. One America is getting richer; the other is not. Let us take inequality as a starting point for our questions about policy making.

Does the system work for everyone, regardless of their income or wealth? According to a pluralistic understanding of American democracy, the answer to this question would be yes.[2] This view holds that government responds to the will of the majority of the people, who make their wishes heard through their votes. Robert Dahl, one of the most esteemed political scientists of the twentieth century, called this system—our system—of governance a "populistic democracy."[3] No one can deny that as a country we do regularly go to the polls and, in all but a few contested cases, the candidate with the most votes takes power. Historically and worldwide, most people have not participated in politics so directly. As Rick from Bainbridge put it when we spoke after the election: "Absolutely I voted; I exercise my American freedom every election."

The key to representation in this system is that voter preferences should not only be polled, but also acted upon through the policy making of the elected officials. Theoretically, some argue that the two-party system encourages candidates to pursue the support of the "median voter": to increase the likelihood of winning elections, candidates necessarily take into account the preferences of average citizens.[4] Scholars have offered evidence to the same effect: policy reflects the will of the majority much of the time.[5] But if our voices are heard, are they heard equally, regardless of our socioeconomic standing? Are we, as Dahl suggested, "political equals"?[6]

There is much reason to be skeptical. Increasingly, statistical analyses of political participation, public opinion, and policy responsiveness indicate that the pluralistic theory of American democracy is not supported today, if it ever was.

Before asking whether votes translate to voice, we might ask who is voting in the first place. Political scientists Schlozman, Verba, and Brady have compiled extensive evidence showing that political engagement is highly unequal. The likelihood of turning out to vote steadily decreases as one moves down the income scale—and that's just the most basic form of political participation. People in the top income bracket are more than twice as likely as those at the bottom to engage in political activities other than voting. One such activity is contributing money to campaigns, which the wealthiest are almost five times more likely to do than the poorest; in addition, of course, the size of the contributions of the wealthiest citizens is much greater that that of other groups. Moreover, the political participation of wealthier Americans is more consistent (they are more likely to participate more often) and more persistent (these patterns hold for decades) than that of other citizens.[7]

There are several reasons why participation and income decline together. The folks I spoke with articulated a couple of them. Paula and Dawn, for example, revealed that their working lives and struggles squeeze out time for other concerns. Others doubt the effectiveness of their participation. When I asked Lisa if she thought the result of the 2012 election would make a difference in her life, she responded: "I would like to think so, but I just don't know anymore. I used to vote all the time, and this time I'm really thinking I'm just not sure if I'm going to." The causes vary, but the outcome is the same. The sounding of political voices is unequal.

Might policy respond to median American voters despite these imbalances in participation? Recent studies give us reason to think not. Instead, they indicate that policy responds differently to the preferences of people in different socioeconomic classes. Leading political scientist Martin Gilens examined the impact of public opinion on nearly two thousand policy issues over the course of thirty years. He found that policy is much more likely to change in response to the preferences of people in higher income brackets than to those in lower income brackets.[8] Similarly, Larry Bartels looked at responsiveness to public opinion in the U.S. Senate, and discovered that the views of the top third of earners in a given constituency receive about 50 percent more weight than those of the middle, while the views of those in the bottom third receive *no weight at all*. Further, Bartels found that Republican senators are about twice as responsive as Democrats to the views of high-income constituents. The parties are equally (but not very) responsive to the views of middle-income constituents, while neither responds to the views of low-income constituents. Bartels concludes gravely that the modern Senate allows for equal representation of incomes rather than citizens.[9]

But let us imagine that, despite these imbalances in participation and responsiveness, policy often still reflects the will of average citizens, as some have found to be true. This paradox can be explained if average Americans share the views of rich Americans.

Helpfully, Gilens addressed this possibility by measuring policy responsiveness when preferences between income groups diverge. He found that when opinions are *not* shared by constituents in the top and bottom income percentiles, government policy is strongly responsive to the views of the top earners and exhibits negligible responsiveness to the views of members of the bottom percentile. The same holds true for divergence between the top and middle percentiles: that is, *responsiveness to median voters is statistically indistinguishable from zero when their preferences diverge from those of the rich.*[10] When an average American does not agree with the rich, her voice simply fails to matter.

What about interest groups? They might, in theory, influence policy in a pluralistic manner. That is, they might reflect and communicate the diverse views held by all citizens. If policy makers respond to these groups, then we could argue that Americans' preferences are fairly represented, even if indirectly rather than through votes.[11] On the other hand, responsiveness to interest groups might be biased in favor of business or resource-rich interests. That is, groups with more money, such as corporations, might have more influence over policy makers than mass-based interest groups.[12]

One groundbreaking study tested all four of these possible influences on government policy—ordinary citizens, affluent citizens, business-oriented interest groups, and mass-based interest groups. Martin Gilens and Benjamin Page found that when each one of these possible influences is examined alone, it appears to have a significant impact on policy changes. The key, however, is to test them all together. When this is done, the independent impact of average citizens falls to *near zero*, while interest groups and economic elites retain their influence. Further, the interest groups that matter most are business-oriented rather than mass-based. Interestingly, Page and Gilens demonstrated that the preferences of average Americans and economic elites do often point in the same direction. This confirms the idea that policy fairly often reflects the preferences of average citizens, even if it does not do so because of their own influence.[13] But on the issues about which the wealthy disagree with everyone else—sometimes the most consequential issues—it is the wealthy who get their way.

Now that we know who policy makers are responding to, we might also ask how this happens. The affluent and organized interests influence policy in a variety of ways. Some of these are straightforward, such as lobbying public officials, sponsoring candidates that share their views, and pouring money into campaign advertising. Other tactics are more subtle and hidden from view, like shaping public opinion through mass media or keeping issues off the political agenda altogether.[14] Theorists have also suggested reasons why the rich so often rule, offering ideas varying from the domination of an entire elite to the influence of individual oligarchs.[15] These intellectual debates will persist as long as there are things to own in the world, and the money to buy them with. For now, we don't need to delve deeply into abstract theories to recognize that the rich significantly impact politics, even in a democratic system like that of the United States. Yet in an era of historic economic inequality, we do need to worry more than ever about the relationship between money and power.

Policy mattered at every moment of the Great Recession and its aftermath. The federal government provided critical life support to millions of Americans through extended unemployment benefits, for instance. At the same time, it helped banks and corporations with even more money, maintained or only minimally reformed the deregulation that sparked the downturn, and presided over a recovery disproportionately enjoyed by the rich. Furthermore, ideologically driven policy makers heralded austerity at a time that was—at the very least—too early in the recovery.

Policy is also significant long before and after recessions. The conclusion of each chapter in this book has brought out a key issue in the stories told and placed it into a wider context. That context is invariably shaped by decades of accumulated decision making or, often, by the neglect thereof. In chapter 2, we looked at the increasingly limited role played by labor unions in national politics. Chapter 3, which focused on job and income loss, allowed us to consider the impact of economic decline on entire communities. In chapter 4, we reflected on the choices women make regarding work and how policy has failed to keep up with their progress. By focusing on youth in chapter 5, we saw how our educational system is no longer leading the nation's labor force into prosperity. In chapter 6, it became clear that our farming and energy policies are not always driven by concern for our national well-being. Finally, chapter 7 allowed a critical reflection on how scarcity can perpetuate present and future financial problems.

The issues confronting Americans run long and deep. In navigating them, we must consider who benefits from policy, how, and why. But that intellectual exercise can lead us to an uncomfortable question: Does the system work for everyone? And this question will be hard to answer in the affirmative. Moreover, answering "no" suggests that problems must be resolved, and action needs to be taken. I do not have easy solutions, and this book does not set out a plan of action. The tasks I have set for myself are to humanize, contextualize, and historicize the issues confronting our society, so that we may think about them with empathy, comprehension, and farsightedness. I have sought to show that Americans' predicaments and achievements are widely shared by their fellow citizens.

As I traveled through the cities, suburbs, and rural areas of Ohio, I encountered many sorts of people. Each brought to the table personal histories, current concerns, and future hopes. Their experiences with the Great Recession were far from uniform. Some suffered traumatic setbacks, others just an uncomfortable nudge. Many were probably unfamiliar with the daily grind of others—in important ways, the life of a black woman in Cleveland is quite distant from that of a white farmer, and not just because of the miles that separate them.

Yet I believe that all of the people I spoke with enjoy more commonalities than differences. These characteristics might sound clichéd, but they are real nonetheless: hard work, love for family, perseverance, and humor. Unfortunately, nearly all these people also shared in their common exposure to the "unwinding," a loss of the security that once buttressed life in America. For some, this exposure was as acute as a lost job, a foreclosure notice, or an unexpected and financially crippling hospital bill; for others, it took the form of a more nebulous but palpable fear of an insecure retirement or declining prospects for children and grandchildren. These exposures are experienced at a deeply personal level. But none of us lives in isolation from others. Our country's course is the sum of individual fates. Where has it led us, who is paving it, and where do we want it to go?

Notes

1. As Ohio Goes

1. George Packer, *The Unwinding: An Inner History of the New America* (New York: Farrar, Straus and Giroux, 2013).
2. Figures are in 2012 dollars and are based on Current Population Survey data. Josh Bivens et al., *The State of Working America,* 12th ed. (Ithaca, NY: Cornell Univ. Press, 2012); Amy Hanauer, *Stuck: State of Working Ohio 2013,* report, 2 Sept. (Cleveland, OH: Policy Matters Ohio, 2013), <http://www.policymattersohio.org/wp-content/uploads/2013/09/WorkingOhio_2013.pdf>.
3. This family would include two parents and two children. U.S. Department of Commerce, Economics and Statistics Administration, *Middle Class in America,* report prepared for the Office of the Vice President of the United States, Middle Class Task Force, Jan. (Washington, D.C.: U.S. Department of Commerce, 2010), 24–25, <http://www.esa.doc.gov/sites/default/files/middleclassreport.pdf>.
4. Claudia Goldin and Lawrence F. Katz, *The Race Between Education and Technology* (Cambridge, MA: Belknap Press, 2008).
5. Joseph E. Stiglitz, *The Price of Inequality: How Today's Divided Society Endangers Our Future* (New York: W. W. Norton & Co., 2012).
6. Emmanuel Saez and Thomas Pikkety, "Income Inequality in the United States, 1913–1998," *Quarterly Journal of Economics* 118, no. 1 (Feb. 2003): 1–39. Tables and figures updated to 2012, <http://eml.berkeley.edu/~saez/>.
7. Emmanuel Saez, "Striking It Richer: The Evolution of Top Incomes in the United States," *Pathways Magazine,* Winter 2008, 1–9 (updated Sept. 2013), <http://eml.berkeley.edu/~saez/saez-UStopincomes-2012.pdf>.
8. Thomas Piketty, *Capital in the Twenty-first Century* (Cambridge, MA: Belknap Press, 2014); see chapter 7.
9. Saez, "Striking It Richer," 3.
10. For a critique of the applicability of the theory of marginal productivity to explaining inequality, see Piketty, *Capital,* 304–8.

11. Jacob S. Hacker and Paul Pierson, *Winner-Take-All Politics: How Washington Made the Rich Richer—and Turned Its Back on the Middle Class* (New York: Simon and Schuster, 2010).
12. Piketty, *Capital*, chs. 9 and 10.
13. Jeffrey A. Winters, *Oligarchy* (New York: Cambridge Univ. Press, 2011), 208–54.
14. Saez, "Striking It Richer," 1.
15. Rakesh Kochhar and Richard Fry, *Wealth Inequality Has Widened along Racial, Ethnic Lines, Since End of Great Recession,* Fact Tank Publications, 12 Dec. (Washington, D.C.: Pew Research Center, 2014), <http://www.pewresearch.org/fact-tank/2014/12/12/racial-wealth-gaps-great-recession/>.
16. Of special note is Piketty, *Capital.*
17. David Nakamura, "Obama Campaigns in Ad-saturated Swing State of Ohio," *Washington Post,* 1 Aug. 2012, <http://www.washingtonpost.com/politics/obama-campaigns-in-ad-saturated-swing-state-of-ohio/2012/08/01/gJQAT3f5OX_story.html>.
18. "Biden: I don't recognize Mitt Romney's America," *The Raw Story,* 30 Sept. 2012, <http://www.rawstory.com/rs/2012/09/30/biden-i-dont-recognize-mitt-romneys-america/>; "Mitt Romney: Obama's Vision for America Is 'Entirely Foreign,'" Fox News Insider (blog), 25 Sept. 2012, <http://foxnewsinsider.com/2012/09/25/mitt-romney-obamas-vision-for-america-is-entirely-foreign/>.

2. The Company Is Your Family

1. The exact figure is 18 percent. Lewis Horner, *Manufacturing in Ohio: A Post-Recession Employment Outlook,* report prepared for the Ohio Department of Job and Family Services, Apr. (Columbus, OH: Office of Workforce Development, Bureau of Labor Market Information, 2013), 9, <http://ohiolmi.com/research/publications/Manufacturing_in_Ohio_2013.pdf>.
2. Innovation Ohio, "The Auto Industry in Ohio" (Columbus, OH: Innovation Ohio, 2012), 1–2, <http://69.195.124.74/~innovby5/wp-content/uploads/2012/06/Auto-Loan-3.pdf>.
3. At the peak of the recession in 2009, the industry hit a record low of 609,900 workers. In 2012, manufacturing in Ohio employed 663,500. Amy Hanauer, *State of Working Ohio 2012,* report, Sept. (Cleveland, OH: Policy Matters Ohio, 2012), 4.
4. PBS, "Timeline: Big Three Automakers' Recent Troubles," *PBS NewsHour,* 10 July 2009, <http://www.pbs.org/newshour/updates/business-jan-june09-auto_timeline_03-30/>.

5. John Avlon, "The Daily Beast Talks with Ford's CEO," The Daily Beast, 16 Oct. 2010, <http://www.thedailybeast.com/articles/2010/10/16/ford-ceo-alan-mulally-on-the-auto-bailout-electric-cars.html>.

6. Joann Muller, "Automakers' Report Card: Who Still Owes Taxpayers Money? The Answer Might Surprise You," *Forbes*, 29 Aug. 2012, <http://www.forbes.com/sites/joannmuller/2012/08/29/automakers-report-card-who-still-owes-taxpayers-money-the-answer-might-surprise-you/>.

7. Mitt Romney, "Let Detroit Go Bankrupt" (editorial), *New York Times*, 18 Nov. 2008, <http://www.nytimes.com/2008/11/19/opinion/19romney.html?_r=2&>; David Horsey, "'GM is alive, Osama is dead' Is Obama's Answer to Republicans," *Los Angeles Times*, 5 Sept. 2012, <http://articles.latimes.com/2012/sep/05/nation/la-na-tt-obamas-answer-20120905>.

8. Logan Timerhoff, "The Auto Industry Rescue by the Numbers," Center for American Progress, 9 Oct. 2012, <http://americanprogress.org/issues/economy/news/2012/10/09/40834/the-auto-industry-rescue-by-the-numbers/>.

9. Hanauer, *State of Working Ohio 2012*, 4.

10. Tyrel Linkhorn, "Chrysler Takes Control of Jeep Wrangler Paint Shop, Will Cost Retirees Jobs," *Blade* (Toledo), 29 Nov. 2012, <http://www.toledoblade.com/Automotive/2012/11/29/Chrysler-takes-control-of-Jeep-Wrangler-paint-shop-will-cost-retirees-jobs.html>.

11. Andrew Seidman, "Obama Administration Favored Union Worker Pensions in GM Bailout, House Republicans Say," *Los Angeles Times*, 23 June 2011, <http://articles.latimes.com/2011/jun/23/business/la-fi-gm-bailout-review-20110623>.

12. Lawrence Mishel, *Unions, Inequality, and Faltering Middle-class Wages*, Issue Brief No. 342 (Washington, D.C.: Economic Policy Institute, 2012), 1.

13. Sharon Silke Carty, James R. Healey, and Chris Woodyard, "UAW Strike Comes as a Shock," *USA Today*, 28 Sept. 2007, <http://usatoday30.usatoday.com/money/autos/2007-09-24-uaw-gm_N.htm>.

14. Mark Binelli, *Detroit City Is the Place to Be* (New York: Metropolitan Books, 2012), 163–64.

15. Doron Levin, "Sizing Up Automotive CEO Pay," CNN Money, 2 July 2012, <http://fortune.com/2012/07/02/sizing-up-automotive-ceo-pay/>; Elliot Blair Smith and Phil Kuntz, "Top CEO Pay Ratios," Bloomberg News, 30 Apr. 2013, <http://go.bloomberg.com/multimedia/ceo-pay-ratio/>.

16. Fiat Chrysler Automobiles (FCA), "Average U.S. Hourly Wage Rate—Chrysler Group LLC," news release, 1 Apr. 2011, <http://media.chrysler.com/newsrelease.do;jsessionid=715A8326FF1E6A5BB2F814DE458A343D?&id=11058&mid=316>.

17. In 1978, the rate was 26.6 percent for blue-collar workers. The union wage premium compares workers with similar experience, education,

region, industry, occupation, and military assistance. Mishel, *Unions*, 3–4.

18. New skilled employees still make about thirty dollars per hour. Fiat Chrysler Automobiles (FCA), "Average U.S. Hourly Wage Rate—Chrysler Group LLC," news release, 1 Apr. 2011, <http://media.chrysler.com/newsrelease.do;jsessionid=715A8326FF1E6A5BB2F814DE458A343D?&id=11058& mid=316>.

19. U.S. Department of Labor, Bureau of Labor Statistics, "Union Membership in Ohio–2013," news release 14-538-CHI, 2 Apr. 2014, <http://stats.bls.gov/regions/midwest/news-release/2014/pdf/unionmembership_ohio_20140402.pdf>.

20. Mishel, *Unions*, 6.

21. U.S. Department of Labor, Bureau of Labor Statistics, "Union Members Summary 2013," news release USDL-15-0072, 24 Jan. 2014, <http://www.bls.gov/news.release/union2.nr0.htm>. See table 5.

22. Ibid., see table 3.

23. *Trailer/Body Builders*, "Layoffs to Hit 10% of Kenworth's Chillicothe Workforce," 13 Apr. 2012, <http://trailer-bodybuilders.com/archive/layoffs-hit-10-kenworth-s-chillicothe-workforce>; *Chillicothe Gazette*, "Kenworth Announces More Layoffs," 23 Dec. 2008, ChillicotheGazette.com, <http://www.chillicothegazette.com/article/20081223/UPDATES01/81223011/Kenworth-announces-more-layoffs?nclick_check=1>; Neha Chamaria, "PACCAR's Smart Moves Should Push Revenue Higher," DailyFinance.com, 29 Mar. 2012, <http://www.dailyfinance.com/2012/03/29/paccars-smart-moves-should-push-revenue-higher/>.

24. Studs Terkel, *Working: People Talk about What They Do All Day and How They Feel about What They Do* (New York: New Press, 2004), xi.

25. Piketty, *Capital*, 39–45.

26. Kathryn L. MacKay, "Notable Labor Strikes of the Gilded Age," personal Web site hosted by Weber State University, n.d., <http://faculty.weber.edu/kmackay/notable_labor_strikes_of_the_gil.htm>.

27. A famous essay, then book, by Werner Sombart sparked decades of discussion. See Werner Sombart, *Why Is There No Socialism in the United States?* trans. C. T. Husbands (1906; White Plains, NY: International Arts and Sciences Press, 1976). For a critical review of the literature that ensued, see Eric Foner, "Why Is There No Socialism in the United States?" *History Workshop* 17 (Spring 1984): 57–80.

28. William G. Domhoff, *Who Rules America*, 4th ed. (Boston: McGraw Hill, 2002), 169–74.

29. Kay Lehman Scholozman et al., *The Unheavenly Chorus* (Princeton, NJ: Princeton Univ. Press, 2012), tables in chs. 11 and 12.

3. Uh-oh, Now What?

1. These figures are from the fourth quarter of 2009. D'Vera Cohn et al., *A Balance Sheet at 30 Months: How the Great Recession Has Changed Life in America* (Social Trends Publications, 30 June) (Washington, D.C.: Pew Research Center, 2010), 23, <http://www.pewsocialtrends.org/files/2010/11/759-recession.pdf>.

2. Scott Pelley, "Economic Storm Batters Ohio Town," CBS News, 20 Dec. 2009, <http://www.cbsnews.com/news/economic-storm-batters-ohio-town/>.

3. Ibid.

4. Ohio, like most states, provides unemployment compensation for a maximum of twenty-six weeks.

5. Cohn et al., *A Balance Sheet,* 17–18.

6. Cassandra Shofar, "City of Painesville Growing Impressively," *News-Herald* (Willoughby, OH), 16 Aug. 2011, <http://www.news-herald.com/general-news/20110816/city-of-painesville-growing-impressively-chart>.

7. Regina Garcia Cano, "Painesville's Hispanic Community Doubles in 10 Years, Multiplies 11 Times Since 1990," Cleveland.com, 24 Oct. 2011, <http://blog.cleveland.com/metro/2011/10/painesvilles_hispanic_communit.html>.

8. John Russo and Sherry Lee Linkon, "The Social Costs of Deindustrialization," in *Manufacturing a Better Future for America,* ed. Richard McCormack (Washington, D.C.: Alliance for American Manufacturing, 2009), 183.

9. Hanauer, *State of Working Ohio 2012,* 2.

10. Median household wealth decreased by 19 percent from 2007 to 2009. Cohn et al., *A Balance Sheet,* 4–8.

11. U.S. Department of Labor, Bureau of Labor Statistics, "Local Area Unemployment Statistics" (Ohio), <http://www.bls.gov/lau/>.

12. Hanauer, *State of Working Ohio 2012,* 5–8.

13. Rana B. Khoury, "Are You Listening Ohio? It's Me, Washington," The Huffington Post, 11 Sept. 2012, <http://www.huffingtonpost.com/rana-b-khoury/are-you-listening-ohio_b_1866984.html>.

14. Nanette Byrnes, "Norwalk Furniture: The Factory That Refused to Die," *Bloomberg Businessweek Magazine,* 23 July 2009, <http://www.businessweek.com/magazine/content/09_31/b4141038545060.htm>.

15. Andrew Higgins, "From China, an End Run around U.S. Tariffs," *Washington Post,* 23 May 2011, <http://www.washingtonpost.com/world/asia-pacific/from-china-an-end-run-around-us-tariffs/2011/05/09/AF3GRl9G_story.html>.

16. The index level in June 2006 was 189.93; the level in June 2009 was 133.19. S&P Dow Jones Indices, "S&P/Case-Shiller U.S. National

Home Price Index," McGraw Hill Financial, S&P Dow Jones Indices LLC, <http://us.spindices.com/indices/real-estate/sp-case-shiller-us-national-home-price-index>.

17. Gary Evans, "Norwalk Says Layoffs Now Permanent," *Furniture Today,* 18 Sept. 2008, <http://www.furnituretoday.com/article/359297-norwalk-says-layoffs-now-permanent>.

18. Byrnes, "Norwalk Furniture."

19. Social Security Administration, "Monthly Statistical Snapshot, July 2013," Aug. 2013, <http://www.socialsecurity.gov/policy/docs/quick-facts/stat_snapshot/2013-07.html>.

20. Disability compensation is also hidden from welfare statistics. When President Bill Clinton reformed the welfare system, he did so in large part by transferring welfare obligations to the states. Disability, however, remained a federal program. State welfare payments, therefore, do not count the disabled among their payees, allowing for an apparent decrease in welfare payments since Clinton's reforms. See Chana Joffe, "Trends with Benefits," *This American Life,* 22 Mar. 2013, <http://www.thisamericanlife.org/radio-archives/episode/490/transcript>.

21. Kathy Ruffing, "The Facts about Disability Insurance," Center on Budget and Policy Priorities, Off the Charts (blog), 25 Mar. 2013, <http://www.offthechartsblog.org/the-facts-about-disability-insurance/>.

22. In 2007, there were 2,190,196 applicants; in 2010, there were 2,935,798. Social Security Administration, "Disabled Worker Beneficiary Statistics by Calendar Year, Quarter, and Month" (table), <http://www.ssa.gov/oact/STATS/dibStat.html>.

23. Matthew W. Brault, *Americans with Disabilities: 2010,* Current Population Reports, P70-131, 27 July (Washington, D.C.: U.S. Department of Commerce, 2012), <https://www.census.gov/newsroom/cspan/disability/20120726_cspan_disability_slides.pdf>.

24. Married women saw their status improve (i.e., rise from a lower income tier to a middle or upper income tier) by 3.6 percent, compared to an increase in income of 0.7 percent for women generally, and of 0.5 percent for unmarried women. Pew Research Center, *The Lost Decade of the Middle Class,* Social Trends Publications, 22 Aug. (Washington, D.C.: Pew Research Center, 2012), 70, <http://www.pewsocialtrends.org/files/2012/08/pew-social-trends-lost-decade-of-the-middle-class.pdf>.

25. In 2011, 73 percent of men belonged to middle or upper income tiers; 68 percent of women could say the same. For a three-person household in 2010, a middle income was between $39,418 and $118,255, as calculated by the Pew Research Center, based upon the Current Population Survey.

26. At the end of 2009, 11.2 percent of American men were unemployed, compared with 8.7 percent of women. Cohn et al., *A Balance Sheet,* 22.

27. Russo and Linkon, "Social Costs of Deindustrialization," 185.

28. Ibid., 183.

29. Ibid., 187.

30. Piketty, *Capital,* 260.

4. Done Everything I Could

1. Tamara Draut and Javier Silva, *Borrowing to Make Ends Meet: The Growth of Credit Card Debt in the '90s,* report, Sept. (New York: Demos, 2003), <http://www.demos.org/sites/default/files/publications/borrowing_to_make_ends_meet.pdf>.

2. In 1980 in the United States, women headed 8,705,000 households. The U.S. population that year was 226,542,199. U.S. Department of Commerce, U.S. Census Bureau, *Statistical Abstract of the United States: 2012,* 131st ed. (Washington, D.C.: U.S. Dept. of Commerce, 2011), <https://www.census.gov/compendia/statab>, table 59. Households, Families, Subfamilies, and Married Couples: 1980 to 2010.

3. Wendy Wang, Kim Parker, and Paul Taylor, *Breadwinner Moms,* Social Trends Publications, 29 May (Washington, D.C.: Pew Research Center, 2013), 4–9, <http://www.pewsocialtrends.org/files/2013/05/Breadwinner_moms_final.pdf>.

4. Joan Entmacher et al., *Insecure and Unequal: Poverty and Income among Women and Families, 2000–2011,* gender analysis report, 17 Sept. (Washington, D.C.: National Women's Law Center, 2012), 4, <http://www.nwlc.org/sites/default/files/pdfs/nwlc_2012_povertyreport.pdf>.

5. See, for example, Ross Perlin, *Intern Nation* (Brooklyn: Verso Books, 2011).

6. Ohio Department of Education, "2013 Performance Index Score Rankings," 22 Jan. 2014, <http://education.ohio.gov/lists_and_rankings>.

7. U.S. Department of Commerce, U.S. Census Bureau, Table DP.1. Profile of General Demographic Characteristics: 2000, May 2001, <http://www2.census.gov/census_2000/datasets/demographic_profile/0_United_States/2kh00.pdf>; U.S. Department of Commerce, U.S. Census Bureau, "State and County Quick Facts: Cleveland Heights, Ohio," June 2014, <http://quickfacts.census.gov/qfd/states/39/3916014.html>.

8. Nikki Ferrell, "42 Teachers Laid Off," Cleveland Heights Patch, 23 Apr. 2013, <http://clevelandheights.patch.com/groups/schools/p/42-teachers-laid-off-by-cleveland-heights-university-9ef17e1ef0#video-14094788>.

9. *Cleveland Magazine,* "Anatomy of Heights High," Cleveland Magazine. com, May 2007, <http://www.clevelandmagazine.com/ME2/dirmod. asp?sid=E73ABD6180B44874871A91F6BA5C249C&nm=Arts+%26+ Entertainment&type=Publishing&mod=Publications%3A%3AArticle&

mid=1578600D80804596A222593669321019&tier=4&id=9D08909
7896D4C02BCF139734C611670>.

10. The overall four-year graduation rate is 75.5 percent. The Cleveland
Heights-University Heights City School District lags behind in meeting
the state's requirements for achievement, meeting only eight of twenty-
seven indicators, most based on subject testing. Ohio Department of
Education, "2011–2012 School Year Report Card: Cleve. Hts.-Univ. Hts.
City School District," 2013, <http://reportcard.education.ohio.gov/
Archives%20TS/043794/043794/043794_2011-2012_DIST.pdf>.

11. Joan Entmacher et al., *Insecure and Unequal,* 4.

12. Ferrell, "42 Teachers Laid Off."

13. Ohio Department of Education, "2011–2012 School Year Report Card:
Paint Valley High School," 2013, <http://reportcard.education.ohio.
gov/Archives%20TS/049510/029025/029025_2011-2012_BUILD.pdf>.

14. Wang, Parker, and Taylor, *Breadwinner Moms,* 1.

15. Ibid., 12–13.

16. Anne-Marie Slaughter, "Why Women Still Can't Have It All," *Atlantic,* 13
June 2012, <http://www.theatlantic.com/magazine/archive/2012/07/
why-women-still-cant-have-it-all/309020/>.

17. Judith Warner, "The Opt-Out Generation Wants Back In," *New York
Times,* 7 Aug. 2013, <http://www.nytimes.com/2013/08/11/magazine/
the-opt-out-generation-wants-back-in.html?pagewanted=all&_r=0>.

18. Damaske points out that black women are the exception to this trend;
irrespective of their class background, 100 percent of black women
expect to work continually. Sarah Damaske, *For the Family? How Class
and Gender Shape Women's Work* (Oxford, UK: Oxford Univ. Press,
2011), 49, 190.

19. Organisation for Economic Co-operation and Development (OECD),
Social Policy Division, Directorate of Employment, Labour and Social
Affairs, *Key Characteristics of Parental Leave Systems,* Apr. 2014, updated
17 Aug. 2015, <http://www.oecd.org/els/soc/PF2_1_Parental_leave_
systems.pdf>, 3–4.

20. International Labour Office, Conditions of Work and Employment
Branch, *Maternity at Work: A Review of National Legislation,* 2nd ed.
(Geneva: International Labour Organization, 2010), <http://www.ilo.
org/wcmsp5/groups/public/---dgreports/---dcomm/---publ/documents/
publication/wcms_124442.pdf>.

21. Annie Finnigan, "Everyone But U.S.: The State of Maternity Leave,"
Working Mother Magazine, Oct. 2011, <http://www.workingmother.
com/best-companies/everyone-us-state-maternity-leave>.

22. Figures based on OECD 2012 indicators. Juliana Herman, Sasha Post,
and Scott O'Halloran, "The United States Is Far Behind Other Countries

on Pre-K," Center for American Progress, 2 May 2013, <http://cdn.amer
icanprogress.org/wp-content/uploads/2013/05/InternationalECEBrief
-2.pdf>.

5. Sweating through Your Boots

1. U.S. Department of Labor, Bureau of Labor Statistics, "America's Youth
   at 25: School Enrollment, Number of Jobs Held, and Labor Market Activity: Results from a Longitudinal Survey," news release, 1 Mar. 2013,
   <http://www.bls.gov/news.release/archives/nlsyth_03012013.pdf>,
   7. This news release concerns a long-duration survey that perfectly fit
   Darnell's case. The release summarized findings from the first fourteen
   annual rounds of the National Longitudinal Survey of Youth, a survey
   of approximately nine thousand young Americans born between 1980
   and 1984; the end data represents their experiences between the ages
   of eighteen and twenty-five.
2. According to a news release from the Bureau of Labor Statistics, "blacks
   with a bachelor's degree or more education were employed 68 percent
   of weeks from ages 18 to 25." The report also noted that "the racial
   employment gap is more pronounced at lower levels of educational
   attainment. From ages 22 to 25, white dropouts spent 61 percent of
   weeks employed and 28 percent of weeks out of the labor force, while
   black dropouts spent 44 percent of weeks employed and 42 percent of
   weeks out of the labor force. This difference is much lower among those
   who hold a bachelor's degree. At the same age, white college graduates spent 13 percent of weeks out of the labor force and 84 percent of
   weeks employed and black college graduates spent 17 percent of weeks
   out of the labor force and 79 percent employed." U.S. Department of
   Labor, Bureau of Labor Statistics, "Employment Experience of Youths:
   Results from a Longitudinal Survey News Release," economic news release USDL-13-0339, 1 Mar. 2013, <http://www.bls.gov/news.release/
   archives/nlsyth_03012013.htm>.
3. See, for instance, Kimberley G. Noble et al., "Family Income, Parental
   Education and Brain Structure in Children and Adolescents," *Nature
   Neuroscience* 18, no. 5 (May 2015): 773–78, <http://www.nature.com/
   neuro/journal/v18/n5/full/nn.3983.html>.
4. The Institute for College Access and Success, "Quick Facts about Student
   Debt," Mar. 2014, The Project on Student Debt, <http://ticas.org/sites/
   default/files/legacy/files/pub/Debt_Facts_and_Sources.pdf>.
5. Consumer Financial Protection Bureau, "Mid-year Snapshot of Private
   Student Loan Complaints," July 2013, <http://files.consumerfinance.
   gov/f/201308_cfpb_complaint-snapshot.pdf>.

6. U.S. Department of Commerce, Economics and Statistics Administration, *Middle Class in America*, 24–25.

7. Demos and Young Invincibles, "The State of Young America: Economic Barriers to the American Dream, The Databook," 2 Nov. 2011, <http://www.demos.org/sites/default/files/publications/SOYA_TheDatabook_2.pdf>. See fig. 2.4.

8. Alisa F. Cunningham and Gregory S. Kienzl, "Delinquency: The Untold Story of Student Loan Borrowing," report, Mar. (Washington, D.C.: Institute for Higher Education Policy, 2011), 5.

9. Ibid. Figures are from 2004 to 2009.

10. Scholastica (Gay) Cororaton, "First-Time Home Buyers: 31 Percent of Residential Buyers," 27 Sept. (Chicago: National Association of Realtors, 2012), Economists' Outlook (NAR blog), <http://economistsoutlook.blogs.realtor.org/2012/09/27/first-time-home-buyers-31-percent-of-residential-buyers/>.

11. Demos and Young Invincibles, "The State of Young America: Economic Barriers to the American Dream, Poll Results," 2 Nov. 2011, <http://www.demos.org/sites/default/files/publications/SOYA_PollResults_2.pdf>, 10. The exact proportion described as the "almost half of young people" who delayed buying a home is 46 percent.

12. Demos and Young Invincibles, "The State of Young America: Economic Barriers to the American Dream, The Databook," 18, fig. 1.12. Underemployment Rate by Age, August 2011. This table uses an unadjusted underemployment rate; data derived from Current Population Survey.

13. Ibid., 3.

14. Jaison R. Abel and Richard Deitz, "Do the Benefits of College Still Outweigh the Costs?" ed. Basit Zafar, *Current Issues in Economics and Finance* (report series of the Federal Reserve Bank of New York) 20, no. 3 (2014): 8.

15. Demos and Young Invincibles, "The State of Young America," 43, fig. 4.4: Share of Young Adults Living at Their Parental Home. The data for this table is derived from the U.S. Census Bureau: Families and Living Arrangements 2010, table AD-1. The exact proportion described by "more than half of eighteen– to twenty-four-year-olds" is 53 percent.

16. Adam Davidson, "It's Official: The Boomerang Kids Won't Leave," *New York Times Magazine*, 20 June 2014, <http://www.nytimes.com/2014/06/22/magazine/its-official-the-boomerang-kids-wont-leave.html>.

17. Kay Hymowitz et al., "Knot Yet: The Benefits and Costs of Delayed Marriage in America," report (Charlottesville, VA: National Marriage Project at the University of Virginia, 2013), 12, 3, 5, <http://nationalmarriageproject.org/wp-content/uploads/2013/04/KnotYet-FinalForWeb-041413.pdf>.

18. Ibid., 6-7. The average age of women during their first childbirth was twenty-five in 2008, up from twenty-three in 1980. Ibid., 6–7, fig. 1. The Great Crossover.

19. Liberty University, "About Liberty," Liberty University Web site, 2014, <http://www.liberty.edu/aboutliberty/>.

20. At the officer level, the proportion of women increases slightly to 16 percent. U.S. Department of Defense, Defense Manpower Data Center, "Active Duty Military Personnel by Rank/Grade (Women Only)," 30 Sept. 2012. Figures are from September 2012.

21. Anna Mulrine, "Pentagon Report: Sexual Assault in the Military Up Dramatically," *Christian Science Monitor,* 19 Jan. 2012, <http://www.csmonitor .com/USA/Military/2012/0119/Pentagon-report-Sexual-assault-in-the-military-up-dramatically>.

22. Cohn et al., *A Balance Sheet,* 51.

23. Goldin and Katz, *Race Between Education and Technology,* 289. See part 2.

24. Ibid., 324.

25. Ibid., 325.

26. For more of Piketty's critique of the theory of marginal productivity, see Piketty, *Capital,* 304–8.

27. Abel and Deitz, "Benefits of College," 3–4.

28. Goldin and Katz, *Race Between Education and Technology,* 350–51.

6. Not a Desk Job

1. U.S. Environmental Protection Agency, *Ag 101: Demographics,* 15 Apr. 2013, <http://www.epa.gov/agriculture/ag101/demographics.html>.

2. U.S. Department of Agriculture, National Agricultural Statistics Service, *2007 Census of Agriculture: Ohio State and County Data,* vol. 1, pt. 35 (Feb. 2009): 186, <http://www.agcensus.usda.gov/Publications/2007/ Full_Report/Volume_1,_Chapter_1_State_Level/Ohio/ohv1.pdf>.

3. U.S. EPA, *Ag 101: Demographics.*

4. Ohio Department of Agriculture, *2011 Annual Report and Statistics,* 2012, <http://www.agri.ohio.gov/divs/Admin/Docs/AnnReports/ODA _Comm_AnnRpt_2011.pdf>, 31; U.S. Department of Agriculture, National Agricultural Statistics Service, *Farms, Land in Farms, and Livestock Operations: 2012 Summary,* Feb. 2013, <http://ofp.scc.wa.gov/ wp-content/uploads/2013/02/FarmLandIn-02-19-2013.pdf>, 4, 9; U.S. EPA, *Ag 101: Demographics.*

5. U.S. Department of Agriculture, Economic Research Service, *Farm Household Well-being: Farm Household Income (Historical),* 11 Feb. 2014, <http:// www.ers.usda.gov/topics/farm-economy/farm-household-well-being/ farm-household-income-(historical).aspx#.U7QpJBaoq2Q>.

6. In 2007, 9 percent of farms accounted for 63 percent of sales. U.S. EPA, *Ag 101, Demographics.*

7. Ohio Department of Agriculture, *2011 Annual Report and Statistics,* 36–37.

8. Rosa Dominguez-Faus et al., "Climate Change Would Increase the Water Intensity of Irrigated Corn Ethanol," *Environmental Science and Technology* 47, no. 11 (23 June 2013), 6034–36.

9. Kay McDonald, "Paying More for Food? Blame the Ethanol Mandate," 20 Aug. 2012, CNN Opinion, CNN.com, <http://www.cnn.com/2012/08/20/opinion/mcdonald-corn-ethanol>.

10. U.S. Department of Agriculture, National Agricultural Statistics Service, *2007 Census of Agriculture: Ohio State and County Data,* Feb. 2009, <http://www.agcensus.usda.gov/Publications/2007/Full_Report/Volume_1,_Chapter_1_State_Level/Ohio/ohv1.pdf, 84.

11. Brian M. Riedl, "Seven Reasons to Veto the Farm Bill," The Heritage Foundation, 12 May 2008, <http://www.heritage.org/research/reports/2008/05/seven-reasons-to-veto-the-farm-bill>.

12. Jim Monke and Renee Johnson, *Actual Farm Bill Spending and Cost Estimates,* 13 Dec. (CRS Report No. RL44195) (Washington, DC: Congressional Research Service, 2010), 6, <http://nationalaglawcenter.org/wp-content/uploads/assets/crs/R41195.pdf>.

13. U.S. Department of Agriculture, Economic Research Service, *Agricultural Act of 2014: Highlights and Implications,* 29 Apr. 2014, <http://www.ers.usda.gov/agricultural-act-of-2014-highlights-and-implications.aspx#.U63EcRaoq2Q>.

14. Wendy Patton, *Low-income Ohioans Face Food Assistance Cut in November,* report, Oct. (Cleveland, OH: Policy Matters Ohio, 2013), 1–2, <http://www.policymattersohio.org/wp-content/uploads/2013/10/SNAP_Oct2013.pdf>; Jason Hart, "Ohio's Reliance on Food Stamps Remains Near Record High," 26 Mar. 2015, Ohio Watchdog.org, <http://watchdog.org/208321/ohio-food-stamps/>.

15. Exhibit text, Youngstown Museum of Industry and Labor, Youngstown, Ohio.

16. "Youngstown, Ohio, Population Characteristics, 1890–2000" (table), Sherry Lee Linkon and John Russo, *Steeltown U.S.A.: Work and Memory in Youngstown* (Lawrence, KS: Univ. Press of Kansas, 2002), 27.

17. Ibid.

18. U.S. Department of Energy, Energy Information Administration, *Ohio: State Profile and Energy Estimates,* 27 Mar. 2014, <http://www.eia.gov/state/?sid=OH>.

19. U.S. Department of Energy, Energy Information Administration, *Annual Coal Report 2012,* Dec. 2013. See "Table 2: Coal Production and Number of Mines by State, County, and Mine Type, 2012," 5–8.

20. Mark Squillace, *The Strip Mining Handbook* (Washington, D.C.: Environmental Policy Institute, 1990), ch. 2.

21. U.S. Department of Energy, Energy Information Administration, *Natural*

Gas: Shale Gas Production, 4 Dec. 2014, <http://www.eia.gov/dnav/ng/NG_PROD_SHALEGAS_S1_A.htm>; Leonardo Maugeri, "The Shale Oil Boom: A U.S. Phenomenon," Discussion Paper 2013-05, June 2013, Belfer Center for Science and International Affairs, Harvard University, 3, <http://belfercenter.ksg.harvard.edu/files/draft-2.pdf>.

22. Paul Stevens, "The 'Shale Gas Revolution': Developments and Changes," Chatham House Briefing Paper, 1 Aug. 2012, Chatham House, the Royal Institute of International Affairs, 2, <http://www.chathamhouse.org/sites/files/chathamhouse/public/Research/Energy%2C%20Environment%20and%20Development/bp0812_stevens.pdf>.

23. Ann M. Harris, interview by Rana B. Khoury, Youngstown State University, Youngstown, OH, 29 July 2013; Henry Fountain, "Disposal Halted at Well after New Quake in Ohio," *New York Times,* 1 Jan. 2012, <http://www.nytimes.com/2012/01/02/science/earth/youngstown-injection-well-stays-shut-after-earthquake.html?_r=0>.

24. See, for example, the documentary work of Josh Fox.

25. Ohio Department of Natural Resources, Division of Oil and Gas Resources, "Utica/Point Pleasant Shale Wells," *Ohio Oil and Gas Well Database,* updated 7 Feb. 2015, <http://oilandgas.ohiodnr.gov/well-information/oil-gas-well-database>.

26. Michael Pollan, *The Omnivore's Dilemma: A Natural History of Four Meals* (New York: Penguin Group, 2006), 60–61.

27. Andrea Murphy, "America's Largest Private Companies 2012," *Forbes,* 28 Nov. 2012, <http://www.forbes.com/sites/andreamurphy/2012/11/28/americas-largest-private-companies-2012/>.

28. Pollan, *Omnivore's Dilemma,* 63.

29. Ibid., 44–45.

30. Ibid., 83.

7. In America, You Pay for Your Teeth

1. David U. Himmelstein et al, "Medical Bankruptcy in the United States, 2007: Results of a National Study," *American Journal of Medicine* 122, no. 8 (2009): 1–4.

2. The Real Home Price Index was set at 100 in 1890; in 1997, quarterly prices averaged 108.55, while in 2006, quarterly prices averaged 194.72. Robert J. Shiller, *Irrational Exuberance* 2nd ed. (Princeton, NJ: Princeton Univ. Press, 2005); see dataset for fig. 2.1, updated in 2009; McGraw Hill Financial, S&P Dow Jones Indices, "S&P/Case-Shiller U.S. National Home Price Index," <https://us.spindices.com/indices/real-estate/sp-case-shiller-us-national-home-price-index>.

3. Some economists called the steep rise in house prices a bubble, even before it popped. That's because they foresaw the unsustainability and

irrationality of a continual increase in prices despite the simultaneous increase in supply. See, for example, Paul Krugman, "That Hissing Sound," *New York Times* 8 Aug. 2005, <http://www.nytimes.com/2005/08/08/opinion/08krugman.html?_r=0>. See also Jonathan R. Laing's interview of Yale economist Robert Shiller, "The Bubble's New Home," *Barron's*, 20 June 2005.

4. George W. Bush, Acceptance Speech, 2004 Republican National Convention, New York, NY, 2 Sept. 2004.

5. U.S. Department of Commerce, U.S. Census Bureau, Table 16: Quarterly Homeownership Rates by Race and Ethnicity of Householder: 1994 to Present, Current Population Survey/Housing Vacancy Survey, 2010, <http://www.census.gov/housing/hvs/data/histtabs.html>.

6. See Shiller, *Irrational Exuberance.*

7. "Where Credit Is Due: A Timeline of the Mortgage Crisis," *Mother Jones,* July/August 2008, <http://www.motherjones.com/politics/2008/07/where-credit-due-timeline-mortgage-crisis>.

8. Supreme Court of Ohio, Case Management Section, table: "New Foreclosure Filings, 2004 through 2008," 11 Feb. 2009, <http://www.supremecourt.ohio.gov/JCS/casemng/ForeclosureFilings.pdf>.

9. Loraine herself actively researches and documents the home sales and trends in her neighborhood, and blogs enthusiastically at "That Woman's Weblog," <http://thatwoman.wordpress.com>.

10. Studs Terkel began the introduction to his celebrated 1974 book *Working* with these unforgettable words: "This book, being about work is, by its very nature, about violence—to the spirit as well as to the body." Studs Terkel, *Working: People Talk About What They Do All Day and How They Feel About What They Do* (1974; New York: New Press, 2004), xi.

11. Carmen DeNavas-Walt, Bernadette D. Proctor, and Jessica C. Smith, "Income, Poverty, and Health Insurance Coverage in the United States: 2012," U.S. Department of Commerce, U.S. Census Bureau Current Population Reports, Sept. 2013, 23–24.

12. Jeffrey Sachs, *The Price of Civilization: Economics and Ethics after the Fall* (London: Bodley Head, 2011), 16. Based on data compiled from the Bureau of Economic Analysis in the U.S. Department of Commerce.

13. Amanda K. Woodrum and Elise Gould, *Getting By in Ohio: The 2013 Basic Family Budget,* July (Cleveland, OH: Policy Matters Ohio, 2013), 1 <http://www.policymattersohio.org/wp-content/uploads/2013/07/FamilyBudget_Jul2013.pdf>. Based on calculations and research from the Economic Policy Institute's Family Budget Calculator.

14. U.S. Department of Commerce, Economics and Statistics Administration, *Middle Class in America,* 24–25.

15. Sendhil Mullainathan and Eldar Shafir, *Scarcity: Why Having Too Little Means So Much* (New York: Times Books, Henry Holt and Co., 2013).

16. Anandi Mani et al., "Poverty Impedes Cognitive Function," *Science* 341, no. 6149 (30 Aug. 2013): 976.

8. So Goes the Nation

1. Dylan Matthews, "Here Is Every Previous Government Shutdown, Why They Happened and How They Ended," *Washington Post*, 25 Sept. 2013, <http://www.washingtonpost.com/blogs/wonkblog/wp/2013/09/25/here-is-every-previous-government-shutdown-why-they-happened-and-how-they-ended/>.

2. The following discussion of theories of American power is guided by the helpful literature review presented in the following essay: Martin Gilens and Benjamin I. Page, "Testing Theories of American Politics," *Perspectives on Politics* 12, no. 3 (Sept. 2014): 564–81.

3. Robert A. Dahl, *A Preface to Democratic Theory* (Chicago: Univ. of Chicago Press, 1956), ch. 2.

4. Anthony Downs, *An Economic Theory of Democracy* (New York: Harper and Row, 1957).

5. See, for instance, Benjamin I. Page and Robert Y. Shapiro, "Effects of Public Opinion on Policy," *American Political Science Review* 77, no. 1 (Mar. 1983): 175–90.

6. Robert A. Dahl, *Polyarchy: Participation and Opposition* (New Haven, CT: Yale Univ. Press, 1971), 1–3.

7. Kay Lehman Schlozman, Sidney Verba, and Henry E. Brady, *The Unheavenly Chorus* (Princeton, NJ: Princeton Univ. Press, 2012).

8. Martin Gilens, *Affluence and Influence: Economic Inequality and Political Power in America* (Princeton, NJ: Princeton Univ. Press, 2012), especially ch. 3.

9. Larry M. Bartels, *Unequal Democracy: The Political Economy of the New Gilded Age* (Princeton, NJ: Princeton Univ. Press, 2008); see especially ch. 9.

10. Gilens, *Affluence and Influence*.

11. David B. Truman, *The Governmental Process: Political Interests and Public Opinion* (New York: Alfred A. Knopf, 1951).

12. E. E. Schattschneider, *The Semisovereign People: A Realist's View of Democracy in America* (New York: Holt, Rinehart, and Winston, 1960).

13. Gilens and Page, "Testing Theories of American Politics."

14. Jeffrey A. Winters and Benjamin I. Page, "Oligarchy in the United States?" *Perspectives on Politics* 7, no. 4 (2009).

15. Paul Sweezy translated Marxian ideas to the American context by identifying class structure as the source of struggle and power, with the ruling class defending private property and the capitalist system. C. Wright Mills expanded the concept of elites to include men from the pinnacles of three

fields: the government, the military, and corporations, arguing that these men predominate in policy making while only sometimes seeking the assent of the masses beneath them. More recently, G. William Domhoff has explored how elites from these different realms could operate in sync with one another, identifying them as a social class connected through their interactions, shared culture, and organizational linkages. Jeffrey Winters counters that economic elites need not coordinate at all; oligarchs translate their material wealth into political influence without acting like a class or holding official governmental positions.

Bibliography

Abel, Jaison R., and Richard Deitz. "Do the Benefits of College Still Outweigh the Costs?" Ed. Basit Zafar. *Current Issues in Economics and Finance* (report series of the Federal Reserve Bank of New York) 20, no. 3 (2014): 1–11.

Avlon, John. "The Daily Beast Talks with Ford's CEO." The Daily Beast. 16 Oct. 2010. <http://www.thedailybeast.com/articles/2010/10/16/ford-ceo-alan-mulally-on-the-auto-bailout-electric-cars.html> (accessed 24 June 2014).

Bartels, Larry M. *Unequal Democracy: The Political Economy of the New Gilded Age.* Princeton, NJ: Princeton Univ. Press, 2008.

"Biden: I don't recognize Mitt Romney's America." The Raw Story, 30 Sept. 2012. <http://www.rawstory.com/rs/2012/09/30/biden-i-dont-recognize-mitt-romneys-america/> (accessed 2 July 2014).

Binelli, Mark. *Detroit City Is the Place to Be: The Afterlife of an American Metropolis.* New York: Metropolitan Books, 2012.

Bivens, Josh, Heidi Shierholz, Lawrence Mishel, and Elise Gould. *The State of Working America,* 12th ed. Ithaca, NY: Cornell Univ. Press, 2012.

Brault, Matthew W. *Americans with Disabilities: 2010.* Current Population Reports, P70-131, 27 July (Washington, D.C.: U.S. Department of Commerce, 2012). <https://www.census.gov/newsroom/cspan/disability/20120726_cspan_disability_slides.pdf> (accessed 24 June 2014).

Bush, George W. Acceptance Speech, 2004 Republican National Convention. New York, NY, 2 Sept. 2004.

Byrnes, Nanette. "Norwalk Furniture: The Factory that Refused to Die." *Bloomberg Businessweek Magazine,* 23 July 2009. <http://www.businessweek.com/magazine/content/09_31/b4141038545060.htm> (accessed 24 June 2014).

Cano, Regina Garcia. "Painesville's Hispanic Community Doubles in Ten Years, Multiplies Eleven Times Since 1990." Cleveland.com, 24 Oct. 2011. <http://blog.cleveland.com/metro/2011/10/painesvilles_hispanic_communit.html> (accessed 24 June 2014).

Carty, Sharon Silke, James R. Healey, and Chris Woodyard. "UAW Strike Comes as a Shock." *USA Today,* 28 Sept. 2007. <http://usatoday30.usatoday.com/money/autos/2007-09-24-uaw-gm_N.htm> (accessed 24 June 2014).

Chamaria, Neha. "PACCAR's Smart Moves Should Push Revenue Higher." Daily Finance.com, 29 Mar. 2012. <http://www.dailyfinance.com/2012/03/29/paccars-smart-moves-should-push-revenue-higher/> (accessed 24 June 2014).

Chillicothe Gazette. "Kenworth Announces More Layoffs," 23 Dec. 2008. Chilli-cotheGazette.com. <http://www.chillicothegazette.com/article/20081223/UPDATES01/81223011/Kenworth-announces-more-layoffs?nclick_check=1> (accessed 24 June 2014).

Cleveland Magazine. "Anatomy of Heights High." Cleveland Magazine.com, May 2007. <http://www.clevelandmagazine.com/ME2/dirmod.asp?sid=E73AB D6180B44874871A91F6BA5C249C&nm=Arts+%26+Entertainemnt&type =Publishing&mod=Publications%3A%3AArticle&mid=1578600D8080459 6A222593669321019&tier=4&id=9D089097896D4C02BCF139734C611670> (accessed 27 June 2014).

Cohn, D'Vera, et al. *A Balance Sheet at 30 Months: How the Great Recession Has Changed Life in America.* Social Trends Publications, 30 June. Washington, D.C.: Pew Research Center, 2010. <http://www.pewsocialtrends.org/files/2010/11 /759-recession.pdf>.

Consumer Financial Protection Bureau. "Mid-year Snapshot of Private Student Loan Complaints," July 2013. <http://files.consumerfinance.gov/f/201308_ cfpb_complaint-snapshot.pdf> (accessed 2 July 2014).

Cororaton, Scholastica (Gay). "First-Time Home Buyers: 31 Percent of Resi-dential Buyers," 27 Sept. (Chicago: National Association of Realtors, 2012), Economists' Outlook (NAR blog). <http://economistsoutlook.blogs.realtor. org/2012/09/27/first-time-home-buyers-31-percent-of-residential-buyers/> (accessed 2 July 2014).

Cunningham, Alisa F., and Gregory S. Kienzl. "Delinquency: The Untold Story of Student Loan Borrowing." Report, Mar. (Washington, D.C.: Institute for Higher Education Policy, 2011), 1–42.

Dahl, Robert A. *Polyarchy: Participation and Opposition.* New Haven, CT: Yale Univ. Press, 1971.

————. *A Preface to Democratic Theory.* Chicago: Univ. of Chicago Press, 1956.

Damaske, Sarah. *For the Family? How Class and Gender Shape Women's Work.* Oxford: Oxford Univ. Press, 2011.

Davidson, Adam. "It's Official: The Boomerang Kids Won't Leave." *New York Times Magazine,* 20 June 2014. <http://www.nytimes.com/2014/06/22/magazine/ its-official-the-boomerang-kids-wont-leave.html> (accessed 2 July 2014).

Demos and Young Invincibles. "The State of Young America: Economic Barriers to the American Dream, The Databook," 2 Nov. 2011. <http://www.demos. org/sites/default/files/publications/SOYA_TheDatabook_2.pdf>.

DeNavas-Walt, Carmen, Bernadette D. Proctor, and Jessica C. Smith. "Income, Poverty, and Health Insurance Coverage in the United States: 2012." U.S. Depart-ment of Commerce, U.S. Census Bureau Current Population Reports, Sept. 2013.

Domhoff, G. William. *Who Rules America: Power and Politics.* 4th ed. Boston: McGraw Hill, 2002.

Dominguez-Faus, Rosa, Christian Folberth, Junguo Liu, Amy M. Jaffe, and Pedro J. J. Alvarez. "Climate Change Would Increase the Water Intensity of Irrigated Corn Ethanol." *Environmental Science and Technology* 47, no. 11 (23 June 2013): 6030–37.

Downs, Anthony. *An Economic Theory of Democracy.* New York: Harper and Row, 1957.

Draut, Tamara, and Javier Silva. *Borrowing to Make Ends Meet: The Growth of Credit Card Debt in the '90s.* Report, Sept. (New York: Demos, 2003). <http://www.demos.org/sites/default/files/publications/borrowing_to_make_ends_meet.pdf> (accessed 27 June 2014).

Entmacher, Joan, Abby Lane, Katherine Gallagher Robbins, and Julie Vogtman. *Insecure and Unequal: Poverty and Income among Women and Families, 2000–2011.* Gender analysis report, 17 Sept. Washington, D.C.: National Women's Law Center, 2012. <http://www.nwlc.org/sites/default/files/pdfs/nwlc_2012_povertyreport.pdf>.

Evans, Gary. "Norwalk Says Layoffs Now Permanent." *Furniture Today,* 18 Sept. 2008. <http://www.furnituretoday.com/article/359297-norwalk-says-layoffs-now-permanent> (accessed 24 June 2014).

Ferrell, Nikki. "42 Teachers Laid Off by Cleveland Heights-University Heights Schools." Cleveland Heights Patch, 23 Apr. 2013. <http://clevelandheights.patch.com/groups/schools/p/42-teachers-laid-off-by-cleveland-heights-university-9ef17e1ef0#video-14094788> (accessed 27 June 2014).

Finnigan, Annie. "Everyone But U.S.: The State of Maternity Leave." *Working Mother Magazine,* Oct. 2011. <http://www.workingmother.com/best-companies/everyone-us-state-maternity-leave> (accessed 11 July 2014). 77–82.

Foner, Eric. "Why Is There No Socialism in the United States?" *History Workshop* 17, no. 1 (Spring 1984): 57–80.

Fountain, Henry. "Disposal Halted at Well after New Quake in Ohio." *The New York Times,* 1 Jan. 2012. <http://www.nytimes.com/2012/01/02/science/earth/youngstown-injection-well-stays-shut-after-earthquake.html?_r=0> (accessed 2 July 2014).

Gilens, Martin. *Affluence and Influence: Economic Inequality and Political Power in America.* Princeton, NJ: Princeton Univ. Press, 2012.

Gilens, Martin, and Benjamin I. Page. "Testing Theories of American Politics: Elites, Interest Groups, and Average Citizens." *Perspectives on Politics* 12, no. 3 (Sept. 2014): 564–81.

Goldin, Claudia, and Lawrence F. Katz. *The Race Between Education and Technology.* Cambridge, MA: Belknap Press, 2008.

Hacker, Jacob S., and Paul Pierson. *Winner-Take-All Politics: How Washington Made the Rich Richer and Turned Its Back on the Middle Class.* New York: Simon and Schuster, 2010.

Hanauer, Amy. *State of Working Ohio 2012.* Report, Sept. Cleveland, OH: Policy Matters Ohio, 2012.

———. *Stuck: State of Working Ohio 2013.* Report, 2 Sept. Cleveland, OH: Policy Matters Ohio, 2013. <http://www.policymattersohio.org/wp-content/uploads/2013/09/WorkingOhio_2013.pdf>.

Herman, Juliana, Sasha Post, and Scott O'Halloran. "The United States Is Far Behind Other Countries on Pre-K." Center for American Progress, 2 May

2013. <http://cdn.americanprogress.org/wp-content/uploads/2013/05/ InternationalECEBrief-2.pdf> (accessed 11 July 2014).

Higgins, Andrew. "From China, an End Run around U.S. Tariffs." *Washington Post,* 23 May 2011. <http://www.washingtonpost.com/world/asia-pacific/ from-china-an-end-run-around-us-tariffs/2011/05/09/AF3GRl9G_story. html> (accessed 24 June 2014).

Himmelstein, David U., Deborah Thorne, Elizabeth Warren, and Steffie Woolhandler. "Medical Bankruptcy in the United States, 2007: Results of a National Study." *The American Journal of Medicine* 122, no. 8 (Aug. 2009): 741–46.

Horner, Lewis. *Manufacturing in Ohio: A Post-Recession Employment Outlook.* Report prepared for the Ohio Department of Job and Family Services, Apr. Columbus, OH: Office of Workforce Development, Bureau of Labor Market Information, 2013. <http://ohiolmi.com/research/publications/Manufacturing_in_Ohio_2013.pdf>.

Horsey, David. "'GM Is Alive, Osama Is Dead' Is Obama's Answer to Republicans." *Los Angeles Times,* 5 Sept. 2012. <http://articles.latimes.com/2012 /sep/05/nation/la-na-tt-obamas-answer-20120905> (accessed 24 June 2014).

Hymowitz, Kay, Jason S. Carroll, W. Bradford Wilcox, Kelleen Kaye. "Knot Yet: The Benefits and Costs of Delayed Marriage in America." Report. Charlottesville, VA: National Marriage Project at the University of Virginia, 2013. <http://nationalmarriageproject.org/wp-content/uploads/2013/04/KnotYet -FinalForWeb-041413.pdf> (accessed 28 July 2014).

Innovation Ohio. "The Auto Industry in Ohio." Columbus, OH: Innovation Ohio, 2012. <http://69.195.124.74/~innovby5/wp-content/uploads/2012/06/Auto -Loan-3.pdf>.

The Institute for College Access and Success. "Quick Facts about Student Debt," Mar. 2014. The Project on Student Debt. <http://projectonstudentdebt.org/ fact_sheets.vp.html> (accessed 2 July 2014).

Joffe, Chana. "Trends with Benefits." *This American Life,* broadcast by Chicago Public Media and Ira Glass, 22 Mar. 2013. <http://www.thisamericanlife. org/radio-archives/episode/490/transcript> (accessed 24 June 2014).

Khoury, Rana B. "Are You Listening Ohio? It's Me, Washington." The Huffington Post, 11 Sept. 2012. <http://www.huffingtonpost.com/rana-b-khoury/are-you-listening-ohio_b_1866984.html> (accessed 24 June 2014).

Kochhar, Rakesh, and Richard Fry. *Wealth Inequality Has Widened along Racial, Ethnic Lines Since End of Great Recession.* Fact Tank Publications, 12 Dec. Washington, D.C.: Pew Research Center, 2014. <http://www.pewresearch. org/fact-tank/2014/12/12/racial-wealth-gaps-great-recession/> (accessed 17 Dec. 2014).

Krugman, Paul. "That Hissing Sound." *The New York Times,* 8 Aug. 2005. <http:// www.nytimes.com/2005/08/08/opinion/08krugman.html?_r=0> (accessed 2 July 2014).

Laing, Jonathan R. "The Bubble's New Home." Interview of Robert Schiller. *Barron's,* 20 June 2005.

Levin, Doron. "Sizing Up Automotive CEO Pay." CNN Money, 2 July 2012. <http://fortune.com/2012/07/02/sizing-up-automotive-ceo-pay/> (accessed 24 June 2014).

Liberty University. "About Liberty." Liberty University Web site, 2014. <http://www.liberty.edu/aboutliberty/> (accessed 2 July 2014).

Linkhorn, Tyrel. "Chrysler Takes Control of Jeep Wrangler Paint Shop, Will Cost Retirees Jobs." The Blade (Toledo), 29 Nov. 2012. <http://www.toledoblade.com/Automotive/2012/11/29/Chrysler-takes-control-of-Jeep-Wrangler-paint-shop-will-cost-retirees-jobs.html> (accessed 24 June 2014).

Livingston, Gretchen. Among 38 Nations, U.S. Is the Outlier When It Comes to Paid Parental Leave. Fact Tank Publications, 12 Dec. Washington, D.C.: Pew Research Center, 2013. <http://www.pewresearch.org/fact-tank/2013/12/12/among-38-nations-u-s-is-the-holdout-when-it-comes-to-offering-paid-parental-leave/> (accessed 11 July 2014).

MacKay, Kathryn L. "Notable Labor Strikes of the Gilded Age." Personal Web site hosted by Weber State University, n.d. <http://faculty.weber.edu/kmackay/notable_labor_strikes_of_the_gil.htm> (accessed 11 July 2014).

Mani, Anandi, Sendhil Mullainathan, Eldar Shafir, and Jiaying Zhao. "Poverty Impedes Cognitive Function." Science 341, no. 6149 (30 Aug. 2013): 976–80.

Matthews, Dylan. "Here Is Every Previous Government Shutdown, Why They Happened and How They Ended." Washington Post, 25 Sept. 2013. <http://www.washingtonpost.com/blogs/wonkblog/wp/2013/09/25/here-is-every-previous-government-shutdown-why-they-happened-and-how-they-ended/> (accessed 8 July 2014).

Maugeri, Leonardo. "The Shale Oil Boom: A U.S. Phenomenon." Discussion Paper 2013-05, June 2013. Belfer Center for Science and International Affairs, Harvard University. <http://belfercenter.ksg.harvard.edu/files/draft-2.pdf>.

McDonald, Kay. "Paying More for Food? Blame the Ethanol Mandate," 20 Aug. 2012. CNN Opinion. CNN.com. <http://www.cnn.com/2012/08/20/opinion/mcdonald-corn-ethanol> (accessed 2 July 2014).

McGraw Hill Financial. S&P Dow Jones Indices."S&P/Case-Shiller U.S. National Home Price Index." <https://us.spindices.com/indices/real-estate/sp-case-shiller-us-national-home-price-index> (accessed 24 June 2014).

Mishel, Lawrence. Unions, Inequality, and Faltering Middle Class Wages. Issue Brief No. 342, Aug. Washington, D.C.: Economic Policy Institute, 2012.

"Mitt Romney: Obama's Vision for America Is 'Entirely Foreign.'" Fox News Insider (blog), 25 Sept. 2012. <http://foxnewsinsider.com/2012/09/25/mitt-romney-obamas-vision-for-america-is-entirely-foreign/> (accessed 2 July 2014).

Monke, Jim, and Renee Johnson. Actual Farm Bill Spending and Cost Estimates, 13 Dec. CRS Report No. RL44195. Washington, DC: Congressional Research Service, 2010. <http://nationalaglawcenter.org/wp-content/uploads/assets/crs/R41195.pdf>.

Mullainathan, Sendhil, and Eldar Shafir. Scarcity: Why Having Too Little Means So Much. New York: Times Books, 2013.

Muller, Joann. "Automakers' Report Card: Who Still Owes Taxpayers Money? The Answer Might Surprise You." *Forbes,* 29 Aug. 2012. <http://www.forbes. com/sites/joannmuller/2012/08/29/automakers-report-card-who-still-owes-taxpayers-money-the-answer-might-surprise-you/> (accessed 24 June 2014).

Mulrine, Anna. "Pentagon Report: Sexual Assault in the Military Up Dramatically." *Christian Science Monitor,* 19 Jan. 2012. <http://www.csmonitor.com/ USA/Military/2012/0119/Pentagon-report-Sexual-assault-in-the-military-up-dramatically> (accessed 2 July 2014).

Murphy, Andrea. "America's Largest Private Companies 2012." *Forbes,* 28 Nov. 2012. <http://www.forbes.com/sites/andreamurphy/2012/11/28/americas-largest-private-companies-2012/> (accessed 2 July 2014).

Nakamura, David. "Obama Campaigns in Ad-saturated Swing State of Ohio." *Washington Post,* 1 Aug. 2012. <http://www.washingtonpost.com/politics/ obama-campaigns-in-ad-saturated-swing-state-of-ohio/2012/08/01/gJQAT-3f5OX_story.html> (accessed 7 Dec. 2014).

Noble, Kimberley G., et al. "Family Income, Parental Education and Brain Structure in Children and Adolescents" *Nature Neuroscience* 18, no. 5 (May 2015): 773–78. <http://www.nature.com/neuro/journal/v18/n5/full/nn.3983.html>.

Ohio Department of Agriculture. *2011 Annual Report and Statistics,* 2012. <http://www.agri.ohio.gov/divs/Admin/Docs/AnnReports/ODA_Comm_ AnnRpt_2011.pdf> (accessed 2 July 2014).

Ohio Department of Education. "2011–2012 School Year Report Card: Cleve. Hts.-Univ. Hts. City School District," 2013. <http://reportcard.education. ohio.gov/Archives%20TS/043794/043794/043794_2011-2012_DIST.pdf> (accessed 27 June 2014).

———. "2013 Performance Index Score Rankings," 22 Jan. 2014. <http:// education.ohio.gov/lists_and_rankings> (accessed 28 July 2014).

Ohio Department of Natural Resources. Division of Oil and Gas Resources. "Utica/Point Pleasant Shale Wells." *Ohio Oil and Gas Well Database,* updated 7 Feb. 2015. <http://oilandgas.ohiodnr.gov/well-information/oil-gas-well-database> (accessed 16 Feb. 2015).

Packer, George. *The Unwinding: An Inner History of the New America.* New York: Farrar, Straus and Giroux, 2013.

Page, Benjamin I., and Robert Y. Shapiro. "Effects of Public Opinion on Policy." *American Political Science Review* 77, no. 1 (Mar. 1983): 175–90.

Patton, Wendy. *Low-income Ohioans Face Food Assistance Cut in November.* Report, Oct. Cleveland, OH: Policy Matters Ohio, 2013. <http://www.policymatters ohio.org/wp-content/uploads/2013/10/SNAP_Oct2013.pdf> (accessed 2 July 2014).

Pelley, Scott. "Economic Storm Batters Ohio Town." CBS News, 20 Dec. 2009. <http://www.cbsnews.com/news/economic-storm-batters-ohio-town/> (accessed 24 June 2014).

Perlin, Ross. *Intern Nation: How to Earn Nothing and Learn Little in the Brave New Economy.* Brooklyn, NY: Verso Books, 2011.

Pew Research Center. *The Lost Decade of the Middle Class.* Social Trends Publica-

tions, 22 Aug. Washington, D.C.: Pew Research Center, 2012. <http://www.
pewsocialtrends.org/files/2012/08/pew-social-trends-lost-decade-of-the-
middle-class.pdf>.

Piketty, Thomas. *Capital in the Twenty-first Century.* Trans. by Arthur Goldham-
mer. Cambridge, MA: Belknap Press, 2014.

Pollan, Michael. *The Omnivore's Dilemma: A Natural History of Four Meals.* New
York: Penguin Group, 2006.

Public Broadcasting Service. "Timeline: Big Three Automakers' Recent Troubles."
PBS Newshour, 10 July 2009. <http://www.pbs.org/newshour/updates/
business-jan-june09-auto_timeline_03–30/> (accessed 24 June 2014).

Riedl, Brian M. "Seven Reasons to Veto the Farm Bill." The Heritage Foundation, 12 May 2008. <http://www.heritage.org/research/reports/2008/05/
seven-reasons-to-veto-the-farm-bill> (accessed 2 July 2014).

Romney, Mitt. "Let Detroit Go Bankrupt." Editorial. *New York Times,* 18 Nov. 2008.
<http://www.nytimes.com/2008/11/19/opinion/19romney.html?_r=2&>
(accessed 24 June 2014).

Ruffing, Kathy. "The Facts about Disability Insurance." Center on Budget and Policy
Priorities. Off the Charts (blog), 25 Mar. 2013. <http://www.offthechartsblog.
org/the-facts-about-disability-insurance/> (accessed 24 June 2014).

Russo, John, and Sherry Lee Linkon. "The Social Costs of Deindustrialization." In
Manufacturing a Better Future for America, ed. Richard McCormack, 187–98.
Washington, D.C.: Alliance for American Manufacturing, 2009.

Sachs, Jeffrey. *The Price of Civilization: Economics and Ethics after the Fall.* London: Bodley Head, 2011.

Saez, Emmanuel. "Striking It Richer: The Evolution of Top Incomes in the
United States." *Pathways Magazine,* Winter 2008: 1–9 (updated Sept. 2013).
<http://elsa.berkeley.edu/~saez/saez-UStopincomes-2012.pdf> (accessed
2 July 2014).

Saez, Emmanuel, and Thomas Pikkety. "Income Inequality in the United States,
1913–1998." *Quarterly Journal of Economics* 118, no. 1 (Feb. 2003): 1–39.
Tables and figures updated to 2012. <http://eml.berkeley.edu/~saez/>
(accessed 2 July 2014).

Schattschneider, E. E. *The Semisovereign People: A Realist's View of Democracy in
America.* New York: Holt, Rinehart, and Winston, 1960.

Schlozman, Kay Lehman, Sidney Verba, and Henry E. Brady. *The Unheavenly
Chorus: Unequal Political Voice and the Broken Promise of American Democracy.*
Princeton, NJ: Princeton Univ. Press, 2012.

Seidman, Andrew. "Obama Administration Favored Union Worker Pensions in GM
Bailout, House Republicans Say." *Los Angeles Times,* 23 June 2011. <http://
articles.latimes.com/2011/jun/23/business/la-fi-gm-bailout-review-20110623>
(accessed 24 June 2014).

Shiller, Robert J. *Irrational Exuberance,* 2nd ed. Princeton, NJ: Princeton Univ.
Press, 2005.

Shofar, Cassandra. "City of Painesville Growing Impressively." *News-Herald* (Willoughby, OH), 16 Aug. 2011. <http://www.news-herald.com/general-news/

20110816/city-of-painesville-growing-impressively-chart> (accessed 24 June 2014).

Slaughter, Anne-Marie. "Why Women Still Can't Have It All." *Atlantic,* 13 June 2012. <http://www.theatlantic.com/magazine/archive/2012/07/why-women-still-cant-have-it-all/309020/> (accessed 27 June 2014).

Smith, Elliot Blair, and Phil Kuntz. "Top CEO Pay Ratios." Bloomberg News, 30 Apr. 2013. <http://go.bloomberg.com/multimedia/ceo-pay-ratio/> (accessed 24 June 2014).

Social Security Administration. "Disabled Worker Beneficiary Statistics by Calendar Year, Quarter, and Month" (table). <http://www.ssa.gov/oact/STATS/dibStat.html> (accessed 24 June 2014).

———. "Monthly Statistical Snapshot, July 2013." Aug. 2013. <http://www.socialsecurity.gov/policy/docs/quickfacts/stat_snapshot/2013–07.html> (accessed 24 June 2014).

Sombart, Werner. *Why Is There No Socialism in the United States?* Trans. C. T. Husbands. 1906; White Plains, NY: International Arts & Sciences Press, 1976.

Squillace, Mark. *The Strip Mining Handbook.* Washington, D.C.: Enviornmental Policy Institute, 1990.

Stevens, Paul. "The 'Shale Gas Revolution': Developments and Challenges." Chatham House Briefing Paper, 1 Aug. 2012. Chatham House, the Royal Institute of International Affairs. <http://www.chathamhouse.org/sites/files/chathamhouse/public/Research/Energy%2C%20Environment%20and%20Development/bp0812_stevens.pdf>, 1–12.

Stiglitz, Joseph E. *The Price of Inequality: How Today's Divided Society Endangers Our Future.* New York: W. W. Norton & Co., 2012.

Supreme Court of Ohio. Case Management Section. Table: "New Foreclosure Filings, 2004 through 2008," 11 Feb. 2009. <http://www.supremecourt.ohio.gov/JCS/casemng/ForeclosureFilings.pdf> (accessed 2 July 2014).

Sweezy, Paul M. *The Theory of Capitalist Development.* New York: Oxford Univ. Press, 1942.

Terkel, Studs. *Working: People Talk About What They Do All Day and How They Feel About What They Do.* New York: New Press, 2004.

Timerhoff, Logan. "The Auto Industry Rescue by the Numbers." Center for American Progress, 9 Oct. 2012. <http://americanprogress.org/issues/economy/news/2012/10/09/40834/the-auto-industry-rescue-by-the-numbers/> (accesesd 24 June 2014).

Trailer/Body Builders. "Layoffs to Hit 10% of Kenworth's Chillicothe Workforce," 13 Apr. 2012. <http://trailer-bodybuilders.com/archive/layoffs-hit-10-kenworth-s-chillicothe-workforce> (accessed 24 June 2014).

Truman, David. *The Governmental Process: Political Interests and Public Opinion.* New York: Alfred A. Knopf, 1951.

U.S. Department of Agriculture. Economic Research Service. *Agricultural Act of 2014: Highlights and Implications,* 29 Apr. 2014. <http://www.ers.usda.gov/agricultural-act-of-2014-highlights-and-implications.aspx#.U63EcRaoq2Q> (accessed 2 July 2014).

———. *Farm Household Well-being: Farm Household Income (Historical)*, 11 Feb. 2014. <http://www.ers.usda.gov/topics/farm-economy/farm-household-well-being/farm-household-income-(historical).aspx#.U7QpJBaoq2Q> (accessed 2 July 2014).

U.S. Department of Agriculture. National Agricultural Statistics Service. *Farms, Land in Farms, and Livestock Operations: 2012 Summary*, Feb. 2013. <http://ofp.scc.wa.gov/wp-content/uploads/2013/02/FarmLandIn-02-19-2013.pdf> (accessed 2 July 2014).

———. *2007 Census of Agriculture: Ohio State and County Data*, Feb. 2009. <http://www.agcensus.usda.gov/Publications/2007/Full_Report/Volume_1,_ Chapter_1_State_Level/Ohio/ohv1.pdf> (accessed 2 July 2014).

U.S. Department of Commerce. Economics and Statistics Administration. *Middle Class in America.* Report prepared for the Office of the Vice President of the United States, Middle Class Task Force, Jan. Washington, D.C.: U.S. Department of Commerce, 2010.

U.S. Department of Commerce. U.S. Census Bureau. *State and County Quick Facts: Cleveland Heights, Ohio*, June 2014. <http://quickfacts.census.gov/qfd/states/39/3916014.html> (accessed 27 June 2014).

———. *Statistical Abstract of the United States: 2012*, 131st ed. Washington, D.C.: U.S. Dept. of Commerce, 2011. <https://www.census.gov/compendia/statab> (accessed 27 June 2014).

———. "Table DP.1. Profile of General Demographic Characteristics: 2000," May 2001. <http://www2.census.gov/census_2000/datasets/demographic_profile/0_United_States/2kh00.pdf> (accessed 27 June 2014).

———. "Table 16: Quarterly Homeownership Rates by Race and Ethnicity of Householder: 1994 to Present." Current Population Survey/Housing Vacancy Survey, 2010. <http://www.census.gov/housing/hvs/data/histtabs.html>.

U.S. Department of Defense. Defense Manpower Data Center. "Active Duty Military Personnel by Rank/Grade (Women Only)," 30 Sept. 2012. <https://www.dmdc.osd.mil/appj/dwp/reports.do?category=reports&subCat=milActDutReg> (accessed 2 July 2014).

U.S. Department of Energy. Energy Information Administration. *Annual Coal Report 2012*, Dec. 2013.

———. *Natural Gas: Shale Gas Production*, 4 Dec. 2014. <http://www.eia.gov/dnav/ng/NG_PROD_SHALEGAS_S1_A.htm> (accessed 16 Feb. 2014).

———. *Ohio: State Profile and Energy Estimates*, 27 Mar. 2014. <http://www.eia.gov/state/?sid=OH> (accessed 22 July2014).

U.S. Department of Labor. Bureau of Labor Statistics. "America's Youth at 25: School Enrollment, Number of Jobs Held, and Labor Market Activity: Results from a Longitudinal Survey." News release USDL-13-0339, 1 Mar. 2013. <http://www.bls.gov/news.release/archives/nlsyth_03012013.pdf>, 1–11.

———. "Local Area Unemployment Statistics" (Ohio). <http://www.bls.gov/lau/> (accessed 24 June 2014).

———. Midwest Information Office. "Union Membership in Ohio—2013." News release 14-538-CHI, 2 Apr. 2014. <http://stats.bls.gov/regions/midwest/

news-release/2014/pdf/unionmembership_ohio_20140402.pdf> (accessed 24 June 2014), 1–6.

———. "Union Members—2013." News release USDL-14-0095, 24 Jan. 2014. <http://www.bls.gov/news.release/archives/union2_01242014.pdf> (accessed 24 June 2014).

U.S. Environmental Protection Agency. *Ag 101: Demographics,* 15 Apr. 2013. <http://www.epa.gov/agriculture/ag101/demographics.html> (accessed 2 July 2014).

Wang, Wendy, Kim Parker, and Paul Taylor. *Breadwinner Moms.* Social Trends Publications, 29 May. Washington, D.C.: Pew Research Center, 2013. <http://www.pewsocialtrends.org/files/2013/05/Breadwinner_moms_final.pdf>.

Warner, Judith. "The Opt-Out Generation Wants Back In." *New York Times,* 7 Aug. 2013. <http://www.nytimes.com/2013/08/11/magazine/the-opt-out-generation-wants-back-in.html?pagewanted=all&_r=0> (accessed 27 June 2014).

"Where Credit Is Due: A Timeline of the Mortgage Crisis." *Mother Jones,* July/August 2008. <http://www.motherjones.com/politics/2008/07/where-credit-due-timeline-mortgage-crisis> (accessed 2 July 2014).

Winters, Jeffrey A. *Oligarchy.* New York: Cambridge Univ. Press, 2011.

Winters, Jeffrey A., and Benjamin I. Page. "Oligarchy in the United States?" *Perspectives on Politics* 7, no. 4 (2009): 731–51.

Woodrum, Amanda K., and Elise Gould. *Getting By in Ohio: The 2013 Basic Family Budget,* July (Cleveland, OH: Policy Matters Ohio, 2013). <http://www.policymattersohio.org/wp-content/uploads/2013/07/FamilyBudget_Jul2013.pdf>.

Index

age differences: in belief in improvement for next generation, 102; in union membership, 28

agriculture: aging of farmers, 108, 110–11; cash-rent and sharecropping in, 59, 112; chestnut farming, 121–23, 127; contribution to economy, 106–7, 113; CSAs in, 120; declining number of farms, 108; dependence on fossil fuels, 129–30; dominance of corn in, 129–30; effects of scale in, 108, 110, 112, 117; energy lease income supporting, 127; energy policies and, 158; families in, 143, 145; farm jobs in, 144–45; farmers' love for, 110–12, 118; government subsidies in, 114–17, 121, 129; markets for, 113–14; toughness of life in, 109–11, 117, 121

Airborne Express, as employer, 39

Akerson, Dan, 27

American Dream, 140; faith in, 4–5, 98–102; lost promise of, 29, 46

Amish communities, 1–2, 122

Appalachia, coal mining in, 123–24

auto industry, 18; executive incomes in, 26–27; government bailout of, 19–20, 46; sexism in, 20–21; unions in, 26, 28, 99; wages and benefits in, 27, 99; wildcat strikes over safety issues, 16–17

bankruptcy: Chrysler, 23; communities filing for, 56; financial institutions filing for, 141; individuals filing for, 134–35, 146

banks: bad loans by, 140–41; foreclosures and, 131–32, 135–36, 141–42; government policies benefiting, 157

Bartels, Larry, 155

Baumhower, Bruce, 23

benefits, 29, 39, 99; loss of, 24–25, 27. *See also* health insurance

Brady, Henry E., 154

Bush, George W., 114

businesses, 2, 15; capital-labor split in, 34–36; influence on government policies, 7, 156–57; trying to mitigate effects of Great Recession, 100–101. *See also* corporations

capital, power of, 35

capital gains, tax rates for, 7

capital-labor split, 34–36

Cargill, dominating corn cycle, 129–30

Carroll County, 121–23, 126–28

child support, 59, 65, 95

Chrysler, 21; employee buyout bid, 17–18; experimenting with outside suppliers, 22–24; government bailout of, 19–20, 23

class, social, 103; influence of, 69, 78–79; unequal political influence of, 154–57

class-consciousness, lack of, 35

Cleveland, poverty in, 81–83, 132

Cleveland Heights, schools in, 70–71

climate change, effects on agriculture, 114

coal mining, 123–24

communities, 56; Amish, 1–2; effects of empty houses in, 138, 142; effects of job losses on, 44, 56–58, 73–75, 158; lack of participation in, 151; pride in, 137–38; quality of schools linked to economy of, 70, 83, 128

Community Supported Agriculture (CSA), 120

unemployment (cont.)
males, 81–82. *See also* jobs: effects of
losses of
unemployment compensation, 40, 42, 157
unions, 15, 29; benefits from, 25, 27, 99;
blamed for decline of manufacturing, 26, 28; decline of, 27–28, 36,
158; members of, 16–18, 26. *See also*
strikes
United Auto Workers (UAW), 17; not
allowed to negotiate for Chrysler employees, 23–24, 26
"unwinding," 3, 159
upward mobility, in American Dream, 4–5
U.S. Army Reserve, 90–91

Verba, Sidney, 154
vulnerability, increasing sense of, 58, 159

wages. *See* incomes
wealth: disparities in, 8, 153, 154–57;
held by top 1 percent, 5–6
women: as caretakers, 77, 86–87; finances of, 55, 72; influences on work
and personal choices of, 78–79, 158;
lack of maternity leave for, 79–80;

maternal leave, lack of, 3, 79–80;
as primary breadwinners, 3, 75–76;
professional and family responsibilities of, 77–79; as single mothers,
59–60, 65–72, 81–82
work, 34; disability related to, 14–16;
family seen as distraction from, 21–
22; gender discrimination in, 20–21;
rewards for, 4–5, 145–46, 148; safety
issues at, 16–17. *See also* jobs
work ethic, 144–45; criticism of young
people's, 32–33, 111, 147
workers: competition between younger
and older, 24–26; power of, 34–35
working class: lack of labor party to represent, 35

young people: accused of lacking work
ethic, 32–33, 111, 147; criticisms of,
32–33, 97; effects of college debt on,
84–85; jobs of, 81–82, 86; moving
back in with parents, 85–88, 146;
optimism of, 29, 102
Youngstown, 125; deindustrialization of,
55–56; steel mills in, 118–19